"A Cthulhu-sized amount of fun. . . . This beastly book is loaded to Dagon's gills with absolutely stunning illustrations . . . a wonder to behold. . . . Lovecraft aficionados will eat up *The Necronomnomnom* . . . literally."
—**Horror Fuel**

"Your must-have guide to Halloween-season eats . . . a side-splitting romp through Lovecraft's oeuvre of oddities. Punnishingly delightful names . . . are sure to please the longtime fan and Lovecraftian neophytes."
—**San Antonio Express-News**

"Absolutely hilarious! . . . This cookbook looks like a work of art. It's beautiful. . . . Great detail was put into making the text sound like it is straight out of one of H. P. Lovecraft's stories."
—**This Geek Loves Food**

"Creepy and spooky. . . . Maybe you're planning a Lovecraft party, or a Halloween party, or you just want a book of spells to read. Either way, you're set with this hefty, well-appointed tome . . . [that has] the ability to chill you to the bone."
—**The Providence Journal**

"A handsome volume, with a beautiful embossed cover and copious illustrations. . . . If you're a Lovecraft fan, this is one you'll want to own."
—**The Steampunk Explorer**

"Wonderful and fun. . . . Not only is the cookbook well produced with great art design, but the content is exceptional. . . . Beautifully done . . . this is an excellent cookbook, and if you are a fan of Lovecraft or just a fan of the macabre, you will love this. If you, like me, are a cookbook collector, this is an indisputable classic that is a must-have."
—**The Well Seasoned Librarian**

The NecroMunchicon

Also by Mike Slater,
Thomas Roache,
and Kurt Komoda

Also by Mike Slater
and Kurt Komoda

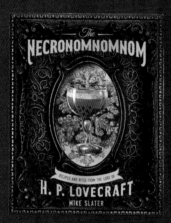

The Necronomnomnom:
Recipes and Rites
from the Lore of
H. P. Lovecraft

Lovecraft Cocktails:
Elixirs & Libations from
the Lore of
H. P. Lovecraft

The
NecroMunchicon

Unspeakable Snacks and Terrifying
Treats from the Lore of

H. P. LOVECRAFT

———•———

MIKE SLATER

EDITED BY THOMAS ROACHE
ILLUSTRATIONS BY KURT KOMODA

Countryman Press

An Imprint of W. W. Norton & Company
Celebrating a Century of Independent Publishing

Copyright © 2023 by Red Duke Games, LLC

For information about permission to reproduce selections from this book, write to Permissions, Countryman Press, 500 Fifth Avenue, New York, NY 10110

For information about special discounts for bulk purchases, please contact W. W. Norton Special Sales at specialsales@wwnorton.com or 800-233-4830

Manufacturing by Toppan Leefung Pte. Ltd.

Book design by Allison Chi

Production manager: Devon Zahn

Countryman Press

www.countrymanpress.com

An imprint of W. W. Norton & Company, Inc.

500 Fifth Avenue, New York, NY 10110

www.wwnorton.com

978-1-68268-795-6

10 9 8 7 6 5 4 3 2 1

This tome is dedicated to the dedicated. We have the most awesome fans, cultists, and devotees we ever could have imagined. You who stop by our booths at shows; who lavish us with praise by email, message, review, and telepathic sending; who commit to video and the Web of Atlach-Nacha offerings of skill and splendor; and who laugh, groan, and titter quietly in your thickly padded . . . reading chairs—this one's for you. Snack sinisterly.

Oh, and the cats. Too many Ultharian references not to include them. Gratitude to Kurt for that idea and their adorably visualized visages.

CTHONTENTS

INTRODUCTION

In the beginning, all was darkness, and the darkness was...peckish, maybe even hangry. Something said, "Let there be snacks!" And it was good. Snacks. We all love them. Game nights, parties, even midnight itself wouldn't be the same without them. In the long list—yes, there's a list—of topics we could have chosen to try next in our library of Dark Culinary Delights, snacks offered the best next challenge. We very much wanted to keep the flavor (ahem) of *The Necronomnomnom* but not simply wash, rinse, and reheat. Oh, the masses widely love the eldritch and Lovecraftian language of the original recipes, to be sure (sometimes more so when that love finds help in the appendix if stuck completing a ritual), and we pay homage to that here, but that's not the secret sauce this time.

Recipes tell a story. Often, they relate the warmth of fresh-baked edible affections from the kitchens of loved ones or distant memories of childhood delights now passed to younger generations. If it's a family recipe, it invariably has a story, so...why not do a book of recipes with stories included? That's a grand idea! We'll get right on that. Oh, wait—you hold it in your hands. Art, fiction, recipes—all mixed together? What madness is this?! Well, see if it works for you. We had a blast putting it together and hope it keeps things fresh without losing any key ingredients.

SHORTCUTS

Take them. By all that's holy—and plenty that definitely isn't—take them! In the words of a certain editor: "Only trust-fund kids are going to eat Tater Tots made from scratch; everyone else buys the 5-pound bag." There is wisdom there. This tome of timely, tasty snackables is *meant* to be easy, relatively quick, and feed EoD Local 412 with minimal muss and fuss and maximum enjoyment. Not everything is simple, though. We have culinary cultists to please, after all, but most dishes are accessible to anyone not afraid of an oven (anymore). Buy the premade pie crusts. Take the easy-mode offering if you like; we've ensured that no power from the Kitchens of Furthest Night will take umbrage. Look to satisfy your guests or spawn, not inscrutable beings from beyond your time and space. They have all the time in the universe. You don't. You need to get fun food on plates and in hungry mouths! Don't exclaim, "It can't be this easy!" Because it can. It is. You're welcome. Direct any consternation about simplicity to Nyarlathotep. *He* likes to make things difficult.

FOOD RELIGIONS

We focused on variety. We scoured the known world, traveled across cultures, and meant to exclude no one deliberately. No starships or portals to Vega were available, though, and the natives there consider riding a Byakhee taboo. That said, if you try hard enough, you can modify almost anything as you see fit. For those of you with restrictions, self-imposed or otherwise, we respect your skill at adaptation. You're used to such labors, so, please, have at it! Post your results and share your impressions on our antisocial media pages. Others in the same realm likely will appreciate your efforts. As always, we have interceded with any jealous and inscrutable intelligences from among the stars or trapped behind Elder Signs on your behalf. Modify to your heart's and stomach's content without fear of being turned into a puddle of eye pudding for your offenses. You'll be fine.

SWEET
MADNESS

ALHAZRED PULL-APARTS

Bazaarly delicious pumpkin treats

SERVES 8 AS A TERRIBLE WARNING TO OTHERS
PREP TIME: 30 MINUTES   TOTAL TIME: 1 HOUR

ACCESSORIES TO DAMNATION

Unsalted butter or cooking spray for greasing

½ cup granulated sugar

2½ teaspoons pumpkin pie spice

Two 16-ounce cans Pillsbury Grands Flaky Layer Honey Butter Biscuits or similar (16 biscuits), refrigerated

4 tablespoons (½ stick) unsalted butter, melted

One 15-ounce can pumpkin pie mix (or pumpkin puree, pumpkin pie spice, and granulated sugar to desired sweetness)

1 cup powdered sugar

4 to 6 teaspoons whole milk

2 teaspoons vanilla extract

THE FORBIDDEN ACTS

⓪ To invoke the power of the Evil Day Star, preheat thine oven to 350°F.

⓪ Anoint an 8-by-12-inch baking sheet with butter or cooking spray.

⓪ In a small bowl, combine the granulated sugar and 2 teaspoons of the pumpkin pie spice.

⓪ Separate the first Grand Cylinder of Dough into 8 biscuits and divide each biscuit into 2 layers for a total of 16 rounds.

⓪ Brush one side of each round with melted butter, then top with pumpkin pie mix, reserving one-quarter of the pie mix for later. Sprinkle the rounds with spice-sugar mixture.

⓪ In the pan, lay the biscuit rounds adjacent to one another, with the pumpkin side facing up in the pan. Stagger them as you stack them so that they overlap enough to hide the vessel within which they lie.

⓪ Separate the second Grand Cylinder into 16 biscuit rounds. Spread the butter, pumpkin pie mix, and spice on four of them. Spread only butter on the other dozen. Stack the Chosen Four with the pumpkin spread in the pan, then cover the dish with the buttered rounds (butter side facing up). Scatter the rest of the spice on top.

⓪ Bake 20 to 30 minutes, until the loaf turns a deep golden brown and the center becomes slightly gooey. Allow to cool for 15 minutes.

⓪ In a small bowl, make the icing. Combine ½ teaspoon pumpkin pie spice, the powdered sugar, milk, and vanilla. Mix until slightly thickened. Add more sugar for thickness and spice for flavor as needed. Drizzle the icing across the dish.

⓪ Carve a man in robes and the tomes and pages he should have known better than to record. Serve and let many hands and mouths rend the effigy of one foolish enough to delve into the forbidden wisdom.

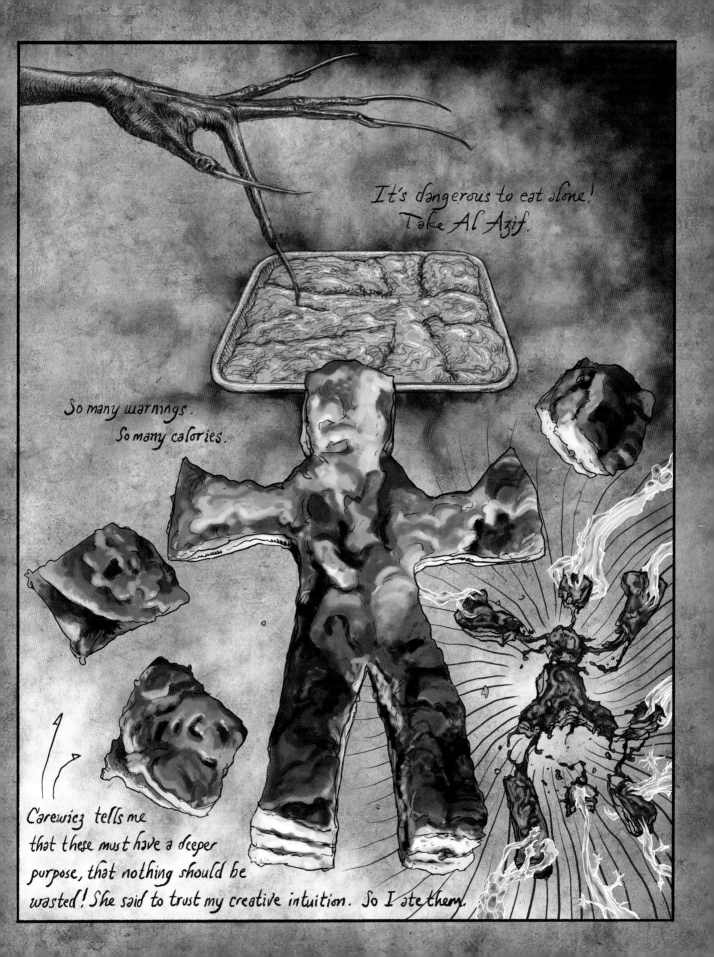

First al-ithnayn

The Merciful One preserves him! Finally, I find him, but al-Muharram is upon us, and I may lay no hand upon him. The mad little poet will not escape my eye, and I shall have what is owed me.

First al-arbi'aa'

The accursed scribbler has seen me. Some hex he threw across the square toward me, and shouted the words no ears given to the All-Hearing should listen to. A fell wind arose then, and the sand did hide him, as all covered their wares and faces against the scouring wind.

Second al-khamees

My coin cannot have gone to his clothes or his belly. He looks like a wretch of parchment-wrapped bones. His eyes are hollow sockets of night's blackness, mere glints within showing that he is not some ghoul arisen from the Nameless City to haunt us. When I confronted him, he only hissed and clutched a tome that bore more skin than he to his breast. He was awaiting Abd al-Malik. Perhaps he seeks to sell to the book merchant and will then have my money. Heaven's Truth, I am nearly inclined to forget his debt in order never to see him again!

Second as-sabt

I swear to the Most Exalted, I sought him not on this day. Yet, there he was, shuddering between two stalls closed for the evening. He lay upon a threadbare rug he would have done better to be praying upon. By His will alone, I left a jug of water by his head. If he dies by morning, I shall take his last possession in recompense, though I am loathe to touch it. A miasma of death clings to him, and I covered my nose and mouth against it. Perhaps the vile tome is worth something. I will take whatever the bookseller offered him for it, though clearly he did not consider it a worthy sum. Perhaps Old Abd was wise enough to want nothing to do with it.

Third al-aHad

He was gone, and I saw no sign he was dragged off. The jug was untouched. He cannot last much longer. Perhaps I shall tell the Caliph's men of his presence here, if they do not already know. Surely there would be some reward for ridding this fine place of his foulness.

Third ath-thulaatha'

At-Tawwaab forgive all my sins! Justice has come! O but how I wished not that upon even one such as him! That was no djinn. Nothing made by the Source of All Goodness walked the market this day. Alhazred's fate was administered by no servant of the King of Kings. Forgive my blasphemy. Its hideousness was too great for me to assign it as part of this Holy Creation. I never will set foot here again.

—Damascene merchant's journal, circa 738 BCE
[translated; collection of MU]

BROWNIE JENKIN

A disturbing yet familiar mug

SERVES KEZIAH MASON, NYARLATHOTEP, AND THE ONE TO WHOM IT IS GIVEN
PREP TIME: 5 MINUTES   TOTAL TIME: 10 MINUTES

THE DARKER HALF

2 tablespoons granulated sugar

2 tablespoons all-purpose flour

1 tablespoon unsweetened cocoa
  powder

1 pinch salt

¼ teaspoon vanilla extract

1½ tablespoons whole milk

1 tablespoon unsalted butter,
  melted

1 tablespoon semi-sweet milk
  chocolate chips

THE (PEANUT) BUTTER HALF

1½ tablespoons granulated sugar

1½ tablespoons all-purpose flour

¼ teaspoon baking powder

1½ tablespoons peanut butter of
  choice

¼ teaspoon vanilla extract

1 tablespoon whole milk

½ tablespoon unsalted butter,
  melted

1 tablespoon semi-sweet milk
  chocolate chips

OPTIONAL SPELL COMPONENTS

Dark chocolate chips

Ice cream of a favored kind

TO BE FUSED IN UNHOLY COMMUNION

0 For each half, mix thee the dry ingredients in separate small bowls, reserving the chocolate chips for last.

0 Add the corresponding wet ingredients to the dry mixtures. Set aside.

0 As each rite is complete in and of itself, thou mayest double one of the halves to make but a single flavor in a single mug. Otherwise, continue at your peril.

0 Cut a piece of parchment paper able to withstand the power of small waves to the diameter of a 12- to 16-ounce mug and place it so the paper cleaves the inner void of the mug into halves.

0 Spoon each prepared mixture into the mug on one side of the paper until each side is full. Reckon ye that the halves remain pure.

0 Gently remove the ancient parchment.

0 Slight mixing may occur during the application of the Waves from on High. Do this for 1 minute 20 seconds, or until the top no longer is wet. Exert the power in controlled bursts of 20 seconds.

0 Your place in the spatial dimensions may alter the time needed, so beware and heed well the exhortations that have gone before.

0 The properly heated mixtures may exceed the dimensions of the vessel. Adorn thy mug with dark fragments or iced cream to serve.

I have followed the instructions faithfully. The scroll warned that "some commixture" of the sections was to be expected, but every time I removed the vessel from the athanor, all I obtained was halves of equal taste and consistency . . . yet the parchment remained whole! How is it possible? How can the properties of the *Arachis hypogaea* and the *Theobroma* intertwine so completely whilst leaving the membrane intact?

Last night I retired early, still ruminating about the problem, and fell asleep reciting a litany of succor to the alchemical demon Echpiel, known to bestow its favors upon worthy supplicants. In my dream, I had the vision of a room, with strange angles and slanted walls. From a corner appeared—flowed—a large beast, looking like a rat with a human face. It walked on its hind legs and carried a sheet of parchment in its paws. I took it, but I could not read the signs written on it. Yet I knew what I was supposed to do. The rat-thing swiped a claw at my hand, and I left a bloody thumbprint on the sheet. Then the beast deftly ripped a piece of the sheet and offered it to me. The dream then became confusing and dark; I recall only the beating of drums, and flames, and screams of terror, and my laughter drowning them.

   This morning, I woke strangely tired, with my clothes in disarray, holding the piece of parchment between my fingers, and with a fresh wound upon my hand. I now know what I shall do.

Success! The dream parchment kept the essences perfectly apart after the process. Ah, this is my Magnum Opus! The alchemical goal of the Two-in-One and the One-with-Two, which Hermes Trismegistus predicted and for which Albertus Magnus strove. . . and I have done it!

   I shall rejoice in my triumph now and worry about the price later.

CAFÉ AU R'LYEH COOKIES

Wafers of the Wakeful Eye: coffee cookies with chocolate ganache flourish

---

YIELDS ONLY TO THE GREATEST POWERS AND 90 COOKIES
PREP TIME: 15 MINUTES **TOTAL TIME:** 40 MINUTES

THE WEIGH OF THE WAFER

10 tablespoons (1¼ sticks) unsalted butter, room temperature

½ cup ghee (clarified butter)

1 cup granulated sugar

1 cup light brown sugar

2 large eggs, room temperature

2½ cups all-purpose flour

¾ cup powdered vanilla nondairy coffee creamer

½ tablespoon baking soda

2 tablespoons instant espresso powder

1 tablespoon Kahlua or other coffee liqueur

TO INVOKE MOCHA·GANACHE

1 cup bittersweet chocolate chips

1 cup semi-sweet chocolate chips

¼ cup heavy cream

1 tablespoon unsalted butter

1 or 2 tablespoons Kahlua or other coffee liqueur

1 cup chocolate-covered espresso beans (optional)

THE WAY OF THE WAFER

0 Preheat the oven to 350°F.

0 With a stand mixer, cream the butter and sugars until light and fluffy.

0 One at a time, add the eggs, mixing until well combined, then add the coffee liqueur.

0 In a bowl, combine the flour, coffee creamer, baking soda, and espresso powder.

0 Slowly add the dry ingredients to the wet ingredients.

0 Line 6 baking sheets with parchment paper.

0 Spoon roughly 1 tablespoon of dough onto the lined sheets, placing them 2 inches apart from one another. Slightly flatten the dough before baking.

0 Bake for 9 to 11 minutes (less time for smaller cookies).

0 While the cookies are cooling, make the Ganaching of Teeth. Into the chamber of twice-boiling over medium heat, combine all the invocations, stirring until smooth.

0 Remove the cookies to cool on a wire rack.

0 Create indentations by pressing a thumb or the back of a spoon into the cookie. Drizzle ganache into the indentations.

0 Optional: Coarsely chop or grind the chocolate-covered beans and sprinkle the fragments onto the ganache. Let the cookies sit for 2 hours, until the ganache sets, then serve.

"What we're seeing here from the News 9 Truth Chopper is unbeliev-able! Masses gathered here on [*static*] beach are wading into the water where what appears to be a giant crowned green . . . mermaid . . . is offering them . . . *cookies*? Yes, Bob, I said 'cookies.' This thing has huge tentacles, and each carries an enormous tray of coffee-colored disks. They, they seem to be decorated with letters or something. Man, I'll tell you, they look and smell delicious. We're going in for a closer l—"

Investigators were unable to find a related news story, though News 9 did place an order for a new helicopter mere days after the date of this story. Several people verified as registered regular polltakers among the News 9 viewers have been questioned, but none remembered or is willing to speak of having seen this broadcast. Missing persons reports for the period are sealed by court order. Something's fishy here, and I'm sure it wasn't the cookies–if they ever existed.

—news report transcript, Internet Archive, found on the Dark Web

CULTIST'S DELIGHTS

One Ring to Drool Them All: bacon-wrapped chocolate cheesecake drops

---

SERVES 6
PREP TIME: 20 MINUTES   **TOTAL TIME:** 1 HOUR

THE LURE OF THE LORE

4 ounces cream cheese, room temperature

2 tablespoons granulated sugar

½ teaspoon ground cinnamon

¾ cup heavy whipping cream, cold

1 to 2 cups semi-sweet dark chocolate chips

1 pound thick-sliced bacon

THE THREE BECOME ONE

① Preheat the oven to 400°F.

① In the wells of Mu-Ffin-Pan, roll the bacon into roughly 2-inch diameter rings. Use picks of tooth to hold the shapes if needed.

① Bake for 15 to 18 minutes until bacon crisps and holds its shape.

① While the bacon cooks, prepare the cheesecake filling. In a small bowl, combine the cream cheese, cinnamon, and sugar and whisk until smooth.

① In a stand mixer or with an immersion blender, whip the heavy cream until fluffy yet stiff peaks form.

① Fold the cream cheese mixture into the whipped cream. Mix thee not excessively or thou shalt lose the fluffiness!

① Remove the bacon from the oven, let it rest for 5 minutes, then move the rings to a paper towel to drain excess drippings. Remove any toothpicks.

① Pipe or spoon the cheesecake fluff into the bacon rings, allowing the excess to blossom from the top of each ring.

① Line a baking sheet or plate with parchment paper, carefully transfer the filled rings onto the paper, and refrigerate for 10 minutes.

① In the microwave, melt the chocolate chips on high for 1 to 2 minutes, stopping every 15 to 20 seconds to stir so the chocolate melts evenly and doesn't scorch like the blood used for inscription in Dark One's tome.

① Dip the chilled-filled bacon rings into the melted chocolate and return them to the parchment paper to cool.

① Refrigerate for 10 more minutes but serve forever!

—Crude effigies of the wanderers.
Crude and delicious.

I have only seen them from a distance whilst riding in a caravan through the Brazic ruins one night. Several of them, spread out over a wide area, all moving westward. They did not appear to take notice of us.

I was told that they wear the sewn-together skins of ghoul, ghast, and even night-gaunt, but mostly that of man, whom their shapeless forms aspire to be ~

By the conjoinment of the Three Holies shall they be seduced.
The amorphosities shall be contained within the sacred flesh.
The divine meat of Heaven sealed by the sweet darkness.
The unbelievers shall dissolve in the saliva called forth from
  their watering mouths.
All shall be consumed.

Notes of Chief Investigator LeGrasse
  The apothecary's report found nothing to help explain
the cult's devotion to these things. He reported the sample
"destroyed," but having seen how even my officers act around
them, I have my doubts.
  The tactic is typical of the cult. Outwardly strange, but
effective. I know they had big plans for these drops. I know
there are more of these people out there. What do they want?
None of them will speak, and we can't hold them forever.
They're obviously not harmful. They themselves partake as
part of the ritual. Apparently, they've tried several times
but never made it to their intended point of distribution
with sufficient (or any) stock left. Their leader just glares
at them.
  We found no written recipe. Other notes reference a tome in
which it can be found, but they appear to have been working
from memory. Probably a precaution. Whoever got ahold of that
recipe could put these to any use they wanted. "Come to the
dark side" indeed. I guess they have more than cookies.
  We know that a couple of these weirdos came off that
steamer from Nepal. Perhaps that's my next lead. I don't
relish so long a trip on so thin a clue. Who knows what I
might find there?

    —parchment seized during a raid on cult compound, central Appalachia, 1911

GAUNT WITH THE CINN-ED

Sweet, crisp treats to tickle your tummy

SERVES 4
PREP TIME: 45 MINUTES **TOTAL TIME:** 1 HOUR

THE SHAPE OF MADNESS

4 flour tortillas
2 tablespoons unsalted butter
Granulated sugar
Ground cinnamon

THE SEA OF DARKNESS

6 ounces Goya dark chocolate
½ cup heavy cream
1 tablespoon agave syrup
1 teaspoon vanilla extract
½ teaspoon ground cinnamon
1 pinch salt

Sliced fruits of choice

TICKLISH PROCEDURE

⓿ For the Waking Nightmare, preheat the oven to 350°F.

⓿ Cut or shape the disks of the small tortas into the terrifying shape of the Nightgaunt.

⓿ Place the cut tortillas on a baking sheet.

⓿ Melt the butter and brush it onto tortilla pieces.

⓿ Sprinkle them with sugar and cinnamon to taste.

⓿ Bake for 8 to 10 minutes or until crisp.

⓿ For the Sea of Darkness, rend the darkness of Goya into small fragments.

⓿ Place the pieces of darkness in a bowl over hot water and melt them.

⓿ Add the cream and syrup and mix until smooth.

⓿ Remove from heat and stir in the vanilla extract, cinnamon, and salt.

⓿ Serve in cups or bowls adorned with bat-winged effigies—and sliced strawberries, apple wedges, or orange sections if you wish.

I do not know if it is this evening indulgence that drives the dreams or the dreams that drive my craving.

While it is absurd to the outsider and uninitiated to assert that an event can or cannot be "real" when writing of the Dreamlands, I can say that, in all of my years at the craft, all of the times I have observed their hideous facelessness, I'd never seen them do this before I dreamed of and then prepared that recipe.

The bat-like shapes are obviously symbolic, as one would expect with dream. The dream significance of lavish ingredients, such as the spice, indicate the strength of the dreamer's vision—and point the way to enhance one's power over the Dreamlands. For this reason, I am generous with the "real" stuff, and I am convinced it has an effect upon reaching the Gate.

The black liquid remains a tantalizing mystery. Because the effigies are dipped in it in the waking world, does this explain why one dreams of them clutching and then dropping one another into it beyond the Gate? Or is their behavior <u>driven</u> by some power of sympathetic dream magic born in the waking world? I've not been able to determine which is true, as the recipe is incomplete and doesn't work without the darksome liquescence. But if it is prepared, it is virtually impossible to exert the will to forego its use. Perhaps it is meant to keep them from trying their usual pranks upon travelers in Dream, by compelling their attention to one another? That seems logical (as such things go) and explanatory. Perhaps it is the horn bowl I seem to choose—consistently and unconsciously—to serve it in. It occurs to me, but I am fearful of trying ivory instead.

I must attempt this with a willing companion or several. Perhaps I shall invite the K brothers, as they regularly report dreams of extreme clarity but with the mark of unreality and parallel logics that mark true dream apart from mere drowsing fantasy. I wonder, though. Will a larger group attract their attention more prominently, or will the glamour hold? It is paramount that we all partake then, lest the ritual consumption protect only those who indulge. How then to observe objectively? Perhaps one of us should volunteer to go without and rely on the others for protection in numbers or adept potence. . . . We all shall partake first, and if nothing is learned, I will raise this theory for consideration of practice. Perhaps the Cats can help. They have a similar ritual, though I bitterly hate to expend what little currency I have left with them. At least they always respect their "treaties."

—extract from a dream journal found during an estate sale in Boston, embossed with initials "R.C."

HOT CTHOCOLATE

Melting, tentacled balls of Cthulhu!

YIELDS APPROXIMATELY 12 BALLS
PREP TIME: 15 MINUTES   **TOTAL TIME:** 40 TO 60 MINUTES

DIMENSIONAL DELICACIES

1 cup heavy whipping cream

1 tablespoon granulated sugar

¼ teaspoon salt

Green food coloring

3 cups white chocolate chips

1 tablespoon mint extract

1 cup dehydrated mini marshmallows

Coconut oil (optional)

2 cups bright purple candy melts

¼ cup light Karo syrup

Green nonpareil sugar balls

Whole milk

THE GREAT GREEN GANACHE STIRS

0. In a saucepan over low heat, combine the heavy cream, sugar, and salt. Mix until the sugar and salt dissolve completely.

0. Add green food coloring until you achieve a deep dark green.

0. Increase the temperature to just below a simmer to warm the green cream. Stir continuously so it doesn't scorch.

0. Once the mixture starts to bubble at the edges, remove the pan from the heat and stir in the white chocolate chips and mint extract, creating a thick, smooth, heavy green ganache. The melting should take about 5 minutes, so be patient. Keep stirring!

0. Once completely combined, pour the green ganache into a heat-proof glass dish and allow it to cool to room temperature.

0. Add the mini marshmallows and stir to mix.

0. Refrigerate the marshmallow'd ganache for 30 to 45 minutes.

SHAPE THE SPHERES

0. Line a baking sheet with parchment paper.

0. With a small ice cream scoop or spoon, scoop up approximately 1½ tablespoons of the chilled ganache.

0. Using your hands, gently but quickly roll the ganache into balls and then place your balls onto the parchment. Sprinkle cold water on your palms to help keep the ganache from crawling up your hands and arms in its quest to subsume you. If your ganache grows too soft, freeze it for 10 minutes to firm it quickly.

0. Refrigerate the balls for 20 minutes.

CONTINUES

Looks horrifying, but sips nicely!

The "star spa--wn."
...
That was one of ol' O.Baer's.
I refuse to be held responsible!

DIP YOUR BALLS IN MADNESS

- In a bowl able to withstand the hellish radiation of short wavelengths, gently warm 1 cup of purple candy melts, according to package instructions, until the candy melts become liquid-smooth and just slightly runny. If you so desire, you may use a double boiler for this part of the ritual instead.

- Depending on the type of candy melt, you can add a little coconut oil (up to 1 teaspoon, ¼ teaspoon at a time) to thin it to the consistency of cream so it coats the back of a spoon.

- Line a large baking sheet with parchment paper.

- One at a time, drop your chilled balls into the melted purple liquid. Use a fork to roll each ball around until fully covered, then remove the ball from the purple bath, shaking off the excess.

- Transfer the coated balls to the parchment-lined sheet and sprinkle them with green nonpareils.

- Refrigerate the decorated balls for 30 minutes or until firm.

SHAPE THE DARKNESS

- Liquefy now the remaining 1 cup of purple candy melts. Thin not the mix!

- Once melted, add the Karo syrup and mix together well. As you mix, the candy melts will start to solidify, taking on the texture of soft-serve ice cream. An oily liquid (cocoa butter) will extract from the mass. At this point, cease thy mixing!

- Pour this gooey mixture onto a large piece of plastic wrap and allow it to cool to room temperature.

- Once cool, knead the mass like a dough. As you knead, the chocolate will reabsorb the cocoa butter and the Karo, and you will end up with a smooth, pliable dough.

- Tear off pieces of this dough and roll out tentacles.

- On a piece of waxed paper, arrange 8 tentacles of chocolate in a star shape.

- Gently press one decorated cocoa ball into the center of this tentacle star to complete one Cocoa'thulu.

CONTINUES

SUMMON THE GREAT DREAMY

◐ Boil 1 cup of whole milk.

◐ Whisper a prayer for forgiveness and plunge one of the Dreamer's effigies into the hot milk.

◐ Stir vigorously 13 times counterclockwise to aide in the merging of dream and reality. As you stir, the shell and tentacles will melt, releasing what lies within. Iä!

I've had enough of Nightgaunts for some time. I tried something else I'd dreamed up. This journal by my bedside is getting a great deal of use lately. I think having regained the Key, as expected, is accelerating the process greatly. I must not become overconfident. Great danger still remains, and many are the rivals who are more adept than I. My influence is nascent; many of the beings that inhabit the Plateau could snuff my flame like a candle.

The requirement to shape these things as they are must be of some moment. I feel fair sure that I would not have stumbled upon them in aimless wanderings here, nor, if I did, find them again by any means.

The milky pools are a'bubble. They are obviously quite hot. Yet these queer little things crawl into them—to their obvious doom—with no hesitation or apparent suffering. At first, I interpreted their splashings as the desperate flailings of beings in pain, like unto sabertoothed cats fallen into tar pits. But, no—they are instead the reveling, almost ecstatic play of toddlers on bath day! Though they visibly are melting into the pools . . . they seem unperturbed. The change in the color of the pools, their relative cooling, and the aroma they release all guided me—with the invulnerability dream provides the self—to sip cautiously from one of them, like a doe bending to lap at a stream while danger still might lurk in the high grass. It also occurred to me that, if this was some form of metamorphosis, "adult" stage organisms might lurk in the pools. . . . But thankfully I never have seen anything emerge from them. My courage held, despite the look of the stuff and my knowledge of what had dropped into what I was about to sample.

It was at the moment, upon first taste, that the knowledge of how to make them in the waking world came to me. At least, that is how it felt to my dream self. It cannot be the other way round, as it is the recipe Etty sent me some years back. I wish I'd tried it sooner so that we could have compared notes. Perhaps we will find each other again, in Kadath or in Leng. In any case, it will be some many nights, I feel, before I understand what instinct draws them to pools, where they come from, and what purpose it all serves. Perhaps when I am not here, disturbing the tableau with my presence, some shy resident of the Dreamlands comes to indulge itself at these pools and upon those who have given themselves up to them. Stranger things have proven the way of things here and probably will again.

—continued extract from a dream journal found during an estate sale in Boston, embossed with initials "R.C."

MACA-RUNES

Inscribed with delight, runes upon 'roons upon 'rons.

YIELDS 24 SIGILICIOUS OBELISKS
PREP TIME: I HOUR 30 MINUTES **TOTAL TIME:** 2 HOURS

THE FOUNDATION STONES

½ cup fine almond flour
1½ tablespoons cocoa powder
2 egg whites, room temperature
I pinch salt
I cup confectioners' sugar

THE SUBSTANCE OF THE PYRAMIDS

2 egg whites, room temperature
I pinch salt
I teaspoon vanilla extract
¼ teaspoon almond extract
⅓ cup granulated sugar
8 ounces shredded coconut

THE INKWELL OF NIGHT

I cup meltable dark chocolate,
   solid at room temperature

BUILD THE FOUNDATION

◐ In a food processor, process the almond flour and cocoa for 3 minutes so it forms a fine powder.

◐ Sift the mixture into a bowl.

◐ In a medium bowl, add the egg whites and salt and beat until frothy.

◐ Add the sugar to the beaten egg whites gradually. Beat for approximately 2 minutes until stiff peaks form.

◐ Gradually fold the dry mixture into the wet mixture and combine. Fold the mixture 40 to 60 turns until the paste holds shapes for 5 to 10 seconds and has the consistency of wet sand.

◐ Line two baking sheets with parchment paper.

◐ Pipe the mix onto the paper in 24 disks about 1½ to 2 inches in diameter.

◐ From a height of 3 inches, drop the tray four times to burst trapped air bubbles and smooth the tops of the cookies.

◐ Let the dough rest at room temperature for 40 to 60 minutes.

◐ Preheat the oven to 300°F.

◐ Bake the dough disks for 16 to 18 minutes. Be still and open not the oven door.

◐ Cool for 5 minutes so the cookies easily pull away from the paper.

YOU MUST CONSTRUCT MORE PYRAMIDS

◐ Preheat the oven to 350°F.

◐ In a medium bowl, add the egg whites and salt and beat until frothy.

CONTINUES

- Add the sugar to the beaten egg whites gradually. Beat for approximately 2 minutes until stiff peaks form.
- Add the remaining Pyramids ingredients and mix until blended evenly.
- Line one baking sheet with parchment paper.
- Form 24 pyramids, each 2 inches tall, and place them on the paper.
- Bake for 14 to 16 minutes until the edges become crispy and brown.

THE INSCRIBING OF THE WARDS

- With a double boiler or in 20-second microwave bursts, melt the dark chocolate.
- Add a dollop of chocolate onto the round side of the macaroon and place the pyramid macaroon onto it.
- Pour the melted chocolate into a piping bag—but not of the Scottish variety!—and pipe the runes (madly) onto a face of each pyramid.
- Refrigerate for at least 10 minutes. When ready, the readers may digest.

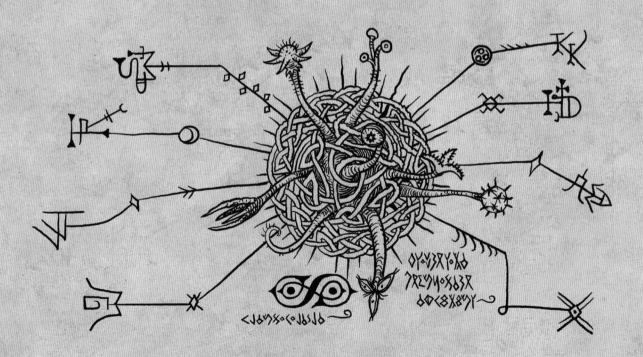

I could be forgiven for thinking they were talismans of some kind at first. The jars we found them in were not unlike the canopic jars of the Egyptians but bore figures wholly unlike their hieroglyphs. Some were Aklo, I'm certain. One, I swear, I have seen in a Parisian cemetery. Regardless, I theorize that they are meant to be consumed—literally—in the process of some ancient magic. Whether it is divinatory, protective, evocational, or otherwise, I have no way of knowing.

The texture is remarkable. The most astounding detail, though, is that they smell and feel as fresh as if they were made this very day. The properties of the jars seem mundane. Simple clay of any of the common Semitic recipes and consistency yet somehow able to preserve their contents for aeons untold. I would not believe it were I not holding one of these strange little pyramids in my own fingers as I write. The aroma is tantalizing, though it might be the height of foolishness to sample something found in this place and for unknown and mystical purpose. I am not the credulous and ignorant fool my rivals have proven to be. The ancients knew more before our cultures were born than all of science can tell us now. The merest example is the perfection of these shapes and their proof against Time itself! Perhaps it is not the jars but the sigils or the composition of these things? I must find a way to sample one without disturbing its integrity or function.

Aldebaran scintillates oddly tonight. The desert wind moans like a winter wolf, though my flag and the fabric of the tent are still as the grave. I have opened all the jars but one. It was a desperate mistake to place all the contents on one of my camp plates to take the photos. Seeing them on tableware like that has my mouth watering, and, though I supped a mere hour ago, a hunger now grips me to which I cannot but assign unnatural agency. In Aldebaran's light, the tiny pyramid with the sigil I've seen before seems to glow.

It moved! By all that's holy—and probably much more that is not—I saw it move! The faintly glowing one has turned toward the Hyades, and a pulse seems to emit from it every few moments. I moved to cover it, and it was like I fought a hurricane wind from some other sky while trying to reach the plate! When I abandoned that course and thought simply to pluck that one from its place, I felt distinctly and specifically allowed to do so.

I fear that I have only moments left and that this will be my last entry. The instant I touched the little pastry, its lure overcame me. I have fed upon the wisdom of something older than Man, and I am not sure which of us has consumed the other.

—found among the blood-stained field notes of Professor Harmon (missing)

MEADISH SWEETBALLS

Hear the boozic of the spheres.

YIELDS 50 BALLS
PREP TIME: 20 MINUTES   **TOTAL TIME:** I HOUR

IN-MEAD-IENTS

I pound ground turkey or chicken
I pound ground beef
I cup plain breadcrumbs
3 eggs
I teaspoon ground ginger
I teaspoon smoked paprika
I cup traditional mead
½ cup unsulfured molasses
½ cup spicy brown mustard

TO CONQUER YOUR HUNGER

0 Preheat the oven to 400°F.

0 In a large bowl, thoroughly combine the ground meats with the breadcrumbs and eggs. If you wish to serve discrete balls, divide the meats, crumbs, and eggs accordingly.

0 Sprinkle in the ginger and paprika, one at a time, and knead until evenly distributed.

0 Line two baking sheets with parchment paper.

0 Roll 50 medium meatballs, roughly 2 inches in diameter, and place them on the parchment.

0 Bake for 15 minutes or until cooked through.

0 In a jar, combine the mead, molasses, and mustard. Seal the lid tightly and shake vigorously to combine.

0 Pour the mead sauce in a wide bowl for dipping or put the meatballs and sauce in a slow cooker on warm 30 minutes before serving. Skaal!

—What I had seen on my journey between the stars was almost certainly an illusion - a cruel trick of the eye! - for I then was afflicted with so desperate a craving for that Svealandic dish!

Damn the government and damn nosey neighbors! Hastur take them both. I'm not running a speakeasy here! Oh, if only they knew what it was. Their minds, such as they are, would melt. That would solve some problems!

Regardless, the sacramental argument won't fly with these narrow-minded fools. I'd put up the trappings of a church they'd recognize if it would help, but my feelings are known too well for that to be convincing. But I think I've found a "solution," if you'll forgive the pun.

[polite cough]

Holes in the law allow for the use of fermented elixirs as *parts of recipes* so long as they are consumed on the premises of a household and not transported elsewhere. Leaving aside the irony, this will serve our need. I have found a method by which we can incorporate the mead into a most delectable snack in the form of tiny meatballs. Borrowing from Scandinavian and Eastern traditions, I have perfected an alchemical immersion specifically for spiced meats. While it works as initially intended, as "dipping sauce," it is even better to let them marinate over low heat. This also skirts any legalistic objection that the sauce constitutes a libation, though, the Yellow King knows, it certainly is. Still, seasoned and viscous as it is, even the solid skulls of our friends in the Agency would be hard-pressed to think it something meant to be consumed alone.

Depending on the constitution of the one partaking, about five of the soaked spheres will ready them for the journey. "Not to leave the premises" indeed!

[maniacal laughter, followed by the mumbling of a second voice]

Yes, yes, it works just as well as the traditional preparation—better even, as one does not arrive as famished as usual! Even the Byakhee seem to enjoy them, though they hardly need them. Mrs. Krapvitz may have seen one through the window before I painted it over. The visit from the Animal Welfare and Health Department was most amusing. That put the police off her further attempts to trouble me for a while, but she is persistent. I think it will be delightful to have her transmuted in a mass of ears and whining lips when I have the means. Perhaps after the next visit. Let the authorities puzzle that out!

[urgent whispering by unidentified second voice]

No, no, professor, you'll be long published and gone from their reach by the time I deal with her. Don't you worry. Just finish that book. Your route to safety from the enemies you will make by this work is well assured. I may even join you.

—transcribed evidentiary statement captured by secret recording

NECRONOMICORN

The Kernels of Corruption

MAKES APPROXIMATELY 12 POPCORN BALLS
PREP TIME: 10 MINUTES   **TOTAL TIME:** 20 MINUTES

SEEDFUL THINGS

Two 3.2-ounce bags plain
   microwave popcorn
¾ cup light corn syrup
4 tablespoons (½ stick) unsalted
   butter, plus more for greasing
2½ cups powdered sugar
I cup dehydrated mini
   marshmallows
Purple food coloring
Purple decorating sugar
Candy eyeball decorations

SUMMON THEM

0 Pop the popcorn and transfer to a large bowl, removing any unpopped kernels.

0 In a medium pot over medium heat, combine the corn syrup, butter, 2 teaspoons cold water, powdered sugar, and marshmallows. Stir until the mixture comes to a boil.

0 Add a few drops of the food coloring until the color pleaseth you.

0 Carefully pour the gooey mixture over the popcorn and stir to coat evenly.

0 Allow the coated popcorn to cool. It should retain enough warmth to shape.

0 Butter your hands and form the popcorn into 3- to 4-inch balls.

0 Fill a large freezer bag with the purple decorating sugar.

0 Place the popcorn balls, while still warm, in the plastic bag and shake vigorously to coat.

0 Remove the sugared popcorn balls and carefully press eyeballs into them, as desired.

0 Lay out a piece of wax paper, transfer the eyes-balls to it, and allow them to cool to room temperature.

0 Wrap the Necronomicorn balls in cellophane or plastic wrap and store at room temperature.

The desert at the base of
Mt. Hatheg-Kla
was not always a desert.

Surely these
aberrations were not
the expected entities!
Baltus should not have attempted
this summoning. The Mad Poet's transcription
was never trustworthy. We were deceived!

Against all reason and sanity, I have removed the curious stone inscribed with the star-shaped variety of what is called the "Elder Sign."

At first, all I observed was a swirl of darksome colors and the curious and sudden smell of . . . baked corn. Sitting quietly, as my eyes adjusted to the purple-tinged light issuing from the still-warm vessel, I began to feel as if it was I who was being observed. I wish I had been—and recorded while at it, for my memory of events is too horrible to recall, yet I am helpless but to recount the tale!

There were more eyes. Many more. I do not know how they could blink and leer as they did, disenfranchised as they were from whatever wretches had donated them. My hands were slick with yellow fat. I shudder to consider where, like the eyes, I had obtained such a thing.

From the warm vessel, I took the bruise-colored nodules and I . . . shaped them. With my fat-slick hands, I pressed and molded them like a godling might form living clay! How they sparkled in that wan light! Glistened! I lost time and self as I reached again and again into the vessel, and I swear to you that I know not how I came to sit before twelve of them, floating blindly before me, demanding "Eyes?" In the tattered shreds of what I now only jokingly can call sleep, I hear their plaintiff, entreating, voiceless voices, "Eyes? Eyes! Eyes?". . . Heaven, forgive me. I gave them to them. In a frenzy, I pressed the eyes into their warm and amorphous flesh. Too many eyes! Eyes on all sides, and still they floated before me, demanding, accusing. "Eyes?"

Against all that is right or could be right, I reached for one, seizing it while it was still disoriented from the sudden gift of sight and—the deep Abyss take me!—I devoured it.

My mind recoils even as my mouth waters at the memory. So sweet! Such flavors and swirling visions that they granted. As I worked my jaw like a mad thing with its snout buried in prey, the others fled. I do not know where. The stone was gone and with it all hope of putting back what I had let loose and given sight beyond sight.

OBED MARSHMALLOWS

"Don't nuke them. They just get bigger!"

SERVES 4 OR 5
TOTAL TIME: 30 MINUTES

THE ANATOMY

12 standard marshmallows

1 large marshmallow

Grenadine

Cocoa Pebbles or similar crunchy
    chocolate cereal

Creamy peanut butter or nut
    butter of choice

13 milk chocolate rectangles

THE PUPIL BECOMES THE MASTER

0 Dip a small sharp knife in grenadine and slice completely through
    all the marshmallows. Glaze the knife for each cut.

0 Insert a rectangle of chocolate between each marshmallow.

0 Microwave the peanut or nut butter for 20 seconds.

0 Cover the curved outsides of the marshmallows (not the flat ends)
    with the peanut butter.

0 Roll the coated marshmallows in the cereal.

0 Dip the tip of the knife into the grenadine and splash it atop the
    marshmallows.

0 On a round plate, arrange the marshmallows in a horrifying pat-
    tern and see whose eyes are bigger than their stomach.

A small pendant from the Olmstead estate. I am told it is of New Zealand origin? Would have thought it a tourist bauble were it not for the Order of Dagon sign carved into its back.

It was a timeworn town, to be sure, somewhat depressed and smelling of brine from the sea cliffs nearby. It seemed steeped in history—but hidden history. At every diner and restaurant, some rubbery-skinned local offered us the "town treat." Their appearance revolted us. They looked like bloodshot goat's eyes covered in fish roe. We refused . . . at first.

Our intended stay was short and cut shorter by our growing discomfort with the locals, but we did find guides to take us to the site of the pirate haunt off the coast. That was why we had come to this forlorn place on our Coast tour, and we meant to see the main attraction!

They were kids really, older teens with a few younger ones mixed in, their leader perhaps twenty. She called them the "the Devil's Reefers." They had their fun and made their coin giving half-credible tours along the coast and out to our destination. I'll say this: They were well-named.

Their skiff—and it was unclear whether they owned or "borrowed" it regularly—reeked of the hand-rolled herbs they all enjoyed. We did not partake . . . well, not directly or intentionally. Perhaps this explains why I was not repelled when our hostess began preparing a plate of the horrid looking "treats." Watching them being prepared, I was much less aghast. Mostly common and some oversized marshmallows, they were. She dipped a wickedly sharp knife in a vial of red liquid and then deftly into one of the white masses. Thumbing a shard of chocolate into the incision made the "wound" all the more convincing. So . . . s'mores with crimson embellishment and no flame? No . . . there was more. The ghastly "roe" affixed to them completed their loathsomeness. For this, she produced a small jar, which she briefly held over the flame of her lighter. Then she coated one of the bloody abominations in it. This is how they got the chocolaty "roe" to stick. The first she handed to my companion, and the second to me. The "Reefers" eyeballed us and then partook of the delight.

Truly, I did not expect such strange alchemy to sit so well on the tongue. With maniacal giggles, they all reached for the remaining treats, wordlessly reserving the largest for their leader. We soon grew as carefree and merry as our guides, though, like the treats themselves, I must attribute that success to the alchemy of location, company, and fare.

—torn page from a diary, found stuffed in the glove compartment
of an abandoned rental car

ARTHUR JERMYN'S CHOCOLATE BANANA BREAD

Satisfy the most primal ape-tites.

SERVES 8 OR MORE
PREP TIME: 10 MINUTES   **TOTAL TIME:** 30 MINUTES

THE TWO LOAVERS COMBINE

5 large bananas, very ripe

2½ tablespoons unsalted butter, melted, plus more at room temperature for greasing

2 large eggs, plus 1 large egg yolk

2 teaspoons vanilla extract

1 cup granulated sugar

2 teaspoons baking soda

1¼ cup all-purpose flour, plus more for dusting

¾ cup cocoa powder

½ teaspoon salt

7 ounces dark chocolate chips

TO BIRTH THE ACCURSED

◐ Preheat the oven to 325°F.

◐ In a large bowl, mash the bananas into a paste, then add the melted butter, eggs, yolk, vanilla extract, sugar, and baking soda. Mix well.

◐ In a small bowl, stir together the flour, cocoa powder, and salt, then use a strainer to sift it into the banana mixture, mixing continuously.

◐ Add most of the chocolate chips, reserving about a tenth, and stir well.

◐ Grease and flour two 9- by 5-inch loaf pans and divide the mixture between them. Make sure it fills the pans no more than half or three-quarters of the way to leave room for rising. Top with the remaining chocolate chips.

◐ Bake for 22 minutes. Test with a toothpick for doneness but be not deceived by the melted chocolate, which will try to deceive you. Better gooey than overdone!

◐ Allow the loaves to cool for a few minutes, then transfer them to a wire rack.

◐ Slice and serve warm with vanilla or orange ice cream.

Sir Alfred Jermyn had an
unnatural passion for bananas.

(x2)

This recipe comes to us from the diary of Jenny Lois, a music-hall entertainer, who for a short time cohabited with Sir Alfred Jermyn. She later mothered his son, Arthur. They shared one of the small, cramped wagons from the traveling circus where they were working. In her diary, Jenny writes about Sir Alfred's unnatural passion for bananas and his uncanny ability to ingest several in one sitting without a hint of discomfort. At first, she mentions it in passing as a curiosity, but in later weeks such a grotesquely abnormal routine repels her. According to the diary, Sir Alfred used to buy bananas in large quantities, always from strange men speaking unfamiliar dialects. After these exaggerated purchases, he sometimes was left with a batch of overripe, unappealing fruit, even after his voracious feeding frenzies. To put those bananas to good use, he created this recipe, which Jenny recorded in her diary.

Several circus workers swear that Sir Alfred used to share this concoction with the enormous gorilla he trained. Some even say that the final clash between them, when the beast smashed Sir Alfred into an unrecognizable pulp, escalated from a previous argument about who should eat the last slice.

After Sir Alfred's bloody demise, Jenny took little Arthur to Jermyn House, his ancestral home. Growing up in a dilapidated manor under severe financial strain, Arthur didn't have many chances to relish this chocolate-rich dessert. But sometimes his mother procured the ingredients, to Arthur's great delight and the consternation of the few remaining servants, who then had to chase him as, in an ecstatic sugar frenzy, he swung acrobatically from the chandeliers to the highest library shelves.

Jenny died in 1911, and Arthur treasured her diary and this recipe until his last day, adjusting it with a few improvements of his own. He seemed to have inherited the prodigious appetites and purchasing habits of his father. From time to time, Arthur baked loaves of chocolate banana bread for himself and the servants.

On August 3, 1913, Arthur Jermyn opened a crate containing horrendous, undeniable proof of his simian lineage and killed himself in an oil-soaked inferno. Only the quick intervention of Soames, the butler, prevented the complete destruction of the manor. Among the items recovered after the blaze, Royal Anthropological Institute professors found one loaf of the dessert and several bunches of overripe bananas. They burned what hadn't already and threw Jenny's diary into a well. Some of them refuse to admit that Arthur Jermyn ever existed.

After those learned men left the house, Soames descended at great personal risk into the garden well and recovered the diary for posterity. Thanks to his efforts, we can enjoy this most excellent treat.

THE GATEAU AND THE KEY LIME

Iä! Choc-Sothoth! Trifle not with this caffeinated trifle!

SERVES 8 TO 12

PREP TIME: 20 MINUTES   **TOTAL TIME:** 3 HOURS

WHAT LURKS BETWEEN

6 Key limes
14 ounces condensed milk
1 cup heavy cream
4 ounces cream cheese
1 tablespoon granulated sugar

THE GATE

2 or 2½ cups strong black coffee, warm
24 ounces rectangular chocolate cookies

DARK MATTER

6 ounces dark chocolate
2 tablespoons unsalted butter, melted

TOPOLOGY OF THE UNIVERSE

½ cup white chocolate
4 or 5 drops purple food dye, fat-soluble
Green frosting pencil (optional)

THE SUMMONING

0 Grate the rinds of the limes and juice them.

0 In a large bowl, combine the condensed milk, heavy cream, lime juice and rinds, cream cheese, and sugar. Stir well until it thickens (but doesn't become too firm). Refrigerate.

0 Procure a flat tray, roughly 8- by 14-inches, that can hold three rows of 8 cookies.

0 Into a wide bowl, pour the coffee.

0 Dunk pairs of chocolate cookies into the coffee for 2 or 3 seconds, remove, drain over the bowl, and lay a 3-by-8 foundation layer of infused cookies on the tray.

0 Spoon a little more coffee atop the foundation layer.

0 Spoon 3 or 4 generous spoonfuls of the chilled lime cream atop the layer and level it with a spatula.

0 Building three more layers of coffee-infused cookies topped with lime cream.

0 When you have covered the fourth layer, spread more lime cream on the sides, creating a frosted gateau with flat sides and top. Refrigerate for at least 2 hours.

0 In a bowl, break the dark chocolate into pieces and gently melt it with indirect heat, over a pot of hot water (*not* boiling).

0 With the same hot-water bath, the microwave, or the underbelly of an enraged hippo, melt the butter.

0 Add the melted butter to the chocolate and gently combine with a spoon.

CONTINUES

obtain Chocolinas

Yog-Sothoth is the Cake and the Key. The Master of all Lime!

With each layer, density changes. Time disappears. All is chaos!

- Spread the molten butter chocolate over the cooled gateau. As it cools, prettify the sides and edges.

- In a small bowl, melt the white chocolate using the same pot of hot water (*not* boiling).

- Add the purple food coloring and stir to dissolve.

- Use a teaspoon to transfer the warm purple chocolate atop the gateau. Combine long surface drags with daring splashes from a few inches high to reproduce the chaotic topology of the universe. Refrigerate for 2 hours, until the cream firms.

- Optional but recommended: With a green frosting pencil, paint a Yog-Sothoth sigil atop the gateau to protect it and all who consume it.

- Slice the gateau into 24 pieces, serve chilled, and pair with coffee.

. . . It was perhaps that which certain secret cults of earth have whispered of as CHOC-SOTHOTH; that which the crustaceans of Mars worship as the Master and Monarch (M&M for short) and carve its manifold-spheroidal likeness into the walls of their underground temples; and which the sucrose brains of the N'stlay spiral nebulae know by the sign of the Gold Roch-Er.

Now the BEING was addressing the entity once called Reese in prodigious waves of intoxicating aromas that were colors and flavors that were sounds.

"Reese," IT seemed to say, "*you wish to sit at the marbled throne in the fabulous city of Her-Shay and from the palace windows contemplate the triangular towers of T'ob-Leeron as their shadows lengthen over the city streets. You want to stroll along the wide avenues of Whon-kha and drink from the inexhaustible fountains that adorn every garden and terrace. You also desire to watch the golden comet of Leendt in the sky as you sip the elixir of the Arabs. But in your heart of hearts, what you really wish is to partake of forbidden confections: the finest delicacies in the Dreamlands, which are not for mortal men. For you, Reese, are not like a child, but you are eager to plunge like a man into the Ultimate secrets, and you burn to know the tart mysteries that dwell between the dimensions of sweetness.*"

With a voice that was his whole mind, the Reese-fragment articulated: "*Yes, that is my desire.*"

The BEING continued. "*What you wish, I am ready to grant, and know that I have granted it only seven times to toqued creatures of your planet. I stand ready to shew you the Truth of the Gateau and the Key Lime, for I AM BOTH. I am Choc-Sothoth. I know the Gateau. I AM the Gateau. I AM the Key Lime and the Guardian of the Gateau. But you can return, if you will it, for the Veil remains unrent before your eyes.*"

—excerpt from *The Dream-Quest of Unknown Khad-Bur'y*

THE
WITCHING SOUR

Mold for edible shotglasses.

Use the straw to slurp out the hidden ~~elixer~~ elixir!

BEASTLY MOONSHOTS

Feast on caged beasts and howl for more!

YIELDS 8 POPS OR 10 TO 12 POPABLES
PREP TIME: 1 MONTH **TOTAL TIME:** 1 MONTH 3 HOURS

PHASES OF THE MOON

Moonshine-infused cherries and
   blueberries

12 ounces white meltable candy
   chips

6 ounces red meltable candy
   chips

6 ounces blue meltable candy
   chips

Chocolate meltable candy chips
   (optional)

WAX PHRENETIC

1. If making moonshine fruit from scratch, soak cherries and blueberries in moonshine or other hard liquor of choice for 1 month.

2. In two pouring cups, carefully melt the candy chips according to package instructions. Use white and red for cherries in one cup and white and blue for blueberries in the other.

3. Into silicone shot glass molds, pour each color half full. Use small molds for popable shots and larger molds for pops. Mix or swirl the colors if desired.

4. Freeze for 1 hour.

5. Remove the half pops/popables from the molds and fill the cavity with infused fruit and as much of the fruit's liquid as desired. No liquid for larger pops is best.

6. Seal the cavities with more melted candy chips or melted chocolate chips, inserting sticks or straws 3 to 4 inches into the pops/popables before the seal hardens.

7. Freeze for 10 minutes.

8. Serve cold.

Consume the smaller popables in one bite. Enjoy the larger, *very* sweet pops more leisurely. The pops can prove messy if they contain a lot of liquid, so use a straw to drink it first! The chocolate variety tastes less sweet, especially with dark chocolate.

OFFICER [REDACTED]: "You acknowledge that you have been advised of your rights?"

SUSPECT: "Yepper."

OFFICER: "You understand what you are being charged with?"

SUSPECT: "Yeah, we run a still. So what? We don't sell nuthin'. Jess fer our own enjoyment. That's legal in small enough amounts. We ain't made more than one cask."

OFFICER: "What's the proof of your . . . distillation?"

SUSPECT: "Couple hunnert 'n' fifty."

OFFICER: "That's not possible. What accounts for the potency?"

SUSPECT: "Family secret." [laughter]

OFFICER: "This goes easier if you cooperate fully."

SUSPECT: "Zat winna face east?"

OFFICER: [pause] "Yes. Why?"

SUSPECT: "Moon'll be up soon. Wanna lemme go?"

OFFICER: "It's Friday evening. You'll be here until Monday morning at the very earliest."

SUSPECT: "Nope. You won't be, neither, you don't take these cuffs off and git gone."

OFFICER: "That sounds like a threat. Why don't you tell me what's in these cylinders and how it's as strong as it is?"

SUSPECT: "Heh, you don' know nuthin' 'bout strong, baw. Whyn 'tchoo bite one open?"

OFFICER: "No, thank you." [sound of something mashed in a metal bowl] "These look like . . . cherries? Is this white chocolate? The liquid is— "

SUSPECT: "—Power! And that's moon dust! And those are—!" [voice distorts, guttural. Sound of metal chair legs squealing on concrete. Shouting, two gunshots. Wet, tearing sounds and screams of pain and animal rage.]

Interrogation room of [redacted] P.D., found smeared with blood. Ragged hole in the external wall under eastern window. Bits of police uniform found clinging to branches and brambles, but neither the suspect nor Officer [redacted] has been seen again. At the time of this report, they have been missing for 29 days. A still was observed, later disassembled and transported to [redacted] in the custody of [redacted]. Several cartons full of light-colored and some dark-colored cylinders recovered. After several days at room temperature, they began to "sweat" a powerful sugar-alcohol condensate. Consumption of the cylinders and their contents deemed "probably safe" . . . in judicious doses.

—transcript of recorded statement of suspect [redacted], Northern Central Ohio, [redacted]

DARK HEARTS OF MARASCHIN-YOH

Cherry bombs burst with power.

SERVES TO CALL THE SORCERER BACK THROUGH TIME, DREAM, AND DIMENSIONS UNTOLD
PREP TIME: 3 DAYS, 10 MINUTES   **TOTAL TIME:** 3 DAYS, 1 HOUR 10 MINUTES

NEEDED COMPOUNDS

25 maraschino cherries, largest you can find

2 ounces coconut Tequila

2 ounces sweet and sour mix

Hershey's Magic Shell or 25 dark chocolate nibs

THE ALCHEMY

0 In a small jar, place 25 cherries.

0 Add equal amounts of Tequila and sour mix to cover the cherries completely.

0 Seal and refrigerate for 3 days.

0 Remove the cherries, reserving the liquid for cocktails or as an adult dessert topping.

0 Plate the cherries and, using a syringe or piping bag, fill their cavities with Hershey Magic Shell. Alternatively, insert dark chocolate cocoa nibs into each cherry.

0 Freeze for 1 hour and serve cold.

Only the earth-realm
has chocolate. Maybe
that's why they keep us
around.

The blood-red orbs
conceal the frigid
blackness within

Maraschin-Yoh
hid his heart in
10,000 things.

Maraschin-Yoh hid his heart
In the Ten Thousand Things
His dark essence he hid from the eye
The blood red orbs concealed
The frigid blackness within him
His power he soaked into the orbs
And they drank his spirit
Red as blood and bright as stars
The ten thousand spheres
Were placed in hidden places
That those who sought his power
Should have to consume
His dark heart
Ten thousand times
And any who did,
Never could contain
What had been divided
Scattered
And shared
His spirit would dwell within
Them all
And down the generations
Again become One
Again would beat
The dark heart of Maraschin-Yoh

—narrow illuminated tablet of jade, found in a copper box,
wrapped in red silk, placed inside a hollowed statue that once formed part of a
pillar taken from a hidden temple standing on the peak of a lost mountain

Some of the older folk I've met in these run-down port towns have lived their entire adult lives prying what seems to be the entirety of their meals from the rocks at low tide.

JNNSMOUTHFULS

A stuffed mushroom dish, courtesy of the half-fish

SERVES FATHER DAGON AND A CABAL OF 8
PREP TIME: I HOUR, FIFTEEN MINUTES   **TOTAL TIME:** I AND ONE HALF HOURS IF SAUTÉING

DRAGGED FROM THE DEPTHS

32 button mushrooms

4 ounces seaweed salad (wakame)

I Ruby Red grapefruit

Balsamic reduction or glaze

THE RITE OF MUTUAL CONSUMPTION

0 From the pallid cups, rip the stalks and discard them.

0 Into each pallid cup, press a generous fingering of the green tendrils. Grant the tendrils freedom to overflow their vessels.

0 Tear the red-pink segments free of their membranes. Separate the segments into ½- to ¼-inch sections.

0 Press these sections atop the green tendrils and seat them firmly.

0 Drip upon them the dark ichor of Ba'alsam and feast!

If the tide is high and you're holding on, sauté the mushrooms in butter, garlic, dry white wine, and freshly ground black pepper before engorging them with the other ingredients.

Foraging in New England

For centuries, residents of the towns and villages along the Atlantic coast of Massachusetts and Southern Maine have kept a wonderful secret. The shores and nearby forests offer veritable heavens for foraging. Early settlers learned, sometimes painfully, which species of wild herbs, berries, weeds, and fungi were safe for consumption. This wisdom they passed to following generations, scribbling it in diaries and cookbooks until today, when coastal New England residents still engage in this life-enriching practice.

The early twentieth century saw a boom in the fishing industry across the region. With it came a sharp increase in pollution of sea and air from waste dumping and fumes emitted from fish factories, though some locals attribute it to bootleg liquor distilleries. To prove their point, they argue that, after the FBI raids of 1927, pollution decreased noticeably and, in only a couple of years, wildlife had recovered completely. Residents reassured this writer that foraged items picked and prepared by an expert are now perfectly safe and impart no discomforting side effects.

Many foraging enthusiasts prize the seemingly inexhaustible seaweed that grows in vast swaths on the marshes. Foragers collect the seaweed, dry it, stack it in sheets, and store it for later use in soups, stews, rice rolls, and other local delicacies.

Not far from the coast, at the foot of immemorial lichened trees untouched by man's ax, a strange type of *Agaricus* button mushroom grows in amazing clusters. They glow with an eerie green phosphorescence, making them easy to pick in the dark. In the same forest grows a wild tree that, when in season, yields succulent fruits with a yellowish rind and a juicy, deep red, sour-sweet pulp.

During my visit to Innsmouth, I made the acquaintance of one Mr. Waite, who graciously gave me a walking tour of the main landmarks of the village, which show signs of decay but also remnants of past glory here and there. When he learned of this article, he insisted on inviting me to lunch at his home, prepared by his wife. She served a heaping serving of glowing mushrooms stuffed with emerald-fresh seaweed and blood-red grapefruit pieces covered in a delicious glaze that I could not identify. Absolutely first-class cuisine made with unsophisticated ingredients that only yesterday were lying on the ground or in the sea. I wanted to give my thanks to Mrs. Waite, who didn't lunch with us, but Mr. Waite said she already had retired to her room.

Back in New York, the memory of those seaweed-filled mushrooms lingers. I have dreamt of them. I can't wait to be in Innsmouth again. The sea is calling me to return.

—from *Wildlife Magazine*, October 1931

LEMONIC POZESTION

When life gives you demons . . .

SERVES 4 WITH A ZESTY APPETITE
PREP TIME: 20 MINUTES   **TOTAL TIME:** 40 MINUTES

SAUCY LEMONIC ICHOR

⅓ cup lemon juice

1 teaspoon vanilla extract

½ cup granulated sugar

Three or four 1-inch pieces fresh djinn-ger root, peeled

1 tablespoon cornstarch

INVITATION TO POZESTION

1⅓ cups all-purpose flour

3 tablespoons granulated sugar

2 tablespoons baking powder

3 teaspoons lemon zest

½ teaspoon salt

1 cup lemonade

1 teaspoon vanilla extract

4 or 5 drops red food coloring

Corn oil for frying

SUMMON THE ICHOR

⓪ In a saucepan over medium-high heat, combine the lemon juice, vanilla extract, sugar, and ginger, mix well, and bring to a boil.

⓪ Into a small glass, add 2 tablespoons of cold water and the cornstarch. Stir to dissolve completely, then add it to the boiling Ichor.

⓪ Stir until the Ichor thickens, approximately 1 minute.

⓪ Remove from heat and allow to cool.

INVITE THE POZESTION

⓪ In a medium bowl, combine the dry ingredients, add the liquids, and mix well to form a batter.

⓪ Heat the corn oil to 350°F.

⓪ In the heated oil, deep-fry 5 or 6 spoonfuls of batter at a time, until golden, approximately 6 minutes if submerged completely or 3 to 4 minutes per side if shallow-frying.

⓪ Remove the lemonic cakes from the oil and transfer them to paper towels to drain.

⓪ When drained, place 5 or 6 lemonic cakes each into four serving glasses.

⓪ Remove the djinn-ger bits from the sauce and drizzle it atop the cakes. Pour the rest of the sauce into a serving bowl for dipping.

⓪ Serve warm and consume with infernally red three-tine cocktail forks.

The devils and demons who inhabit
the hellscapes I have seen did not fall
from anywhere. They writhed and clawed their ascent
from the darkest fathoms from all the nightmares of anything that ever knew terror.

Here is my confession. Do not blame anyone else but me for what I am now going to do. I know for a fact that there is an afterlife and that I am doomed for eternity.

It was the hottest day of a hot summer. The sun burned relentless, not a whisper of wind or cloud on the horizon. Every store in the village was closed until late afternoon, for everyone with sense was napping with fans at top speed or, if they were lucky, air conditioners cranked on high.

I had neither. The power had been cut days ago. The ice block I bought in the morning already had melted on the dead fridge. I was dying for a cold drink. Not alcohol, no. I was half-crazed from the heat, and in my madness and despair, I yelled, "I'd sell my soul for a lemonade!"

"That can be arranged," whispered a voice from a corner of the room. There He was, the Prince of Lies, in the flesh, looking like a regular fellow, but his eyes were unmistakable.

I wasn't scared. I'm a good liar myself. So with parched lips and a feverish head, I prepared to bargain. His offer came simple and nonnegotiable: a lifetime supply of the best lemonade in Hell, the same consumed by Satan and his cohorts on particularly hot days—in return for my shriveled soul.

I didn't believe in the afterlife then—oh, I do now—and anyway, if I was wrong, my past deeds surely hadn't granted me entry to Heaven. So I agreed. He offered no contract to sign in blood.

"Oh, I stopped doing that in the 1800s," he said. Just a handshake between gentlemen, and with that he was gone in a proverbial puff of smoke. Only his grin lingered in the gloom for a moment.

A box materialized on the kitchen table, red and sealed with a sticker of a cloven hoof. I selected my tallest glass and tore the seal.

Ah, Lord of Swindles . . . I should have guessed . . . deep-fried lemonade pancakes? Still hot from the kitchens of Hell?

Stick a fork in me. I'm done.

MORGUEARITA SLABS

Zest in piece with no-bake cheesecake bites.

SERVES A DOZEN OF THEM RIGHT
PREP TIME: 10 MINUTES   **TOTAL TIME:** 3 HOURS 40 MINUTES

IN THE TOMBS

20 graham crackers, 2½ inches square

Cooking spray

½ teaspoon ground cinnamon

¼ cup honey

3 tablespoons unsalted butter, melted

2 tablespoons orange juice

¼ ounce unflavored gelatin

2 limes

32 ounces cream cheese, room temperature

1 cup granulated sugar

¾ cup sour cream

¼ cup Tequila of choice

¼ cup lime juice

Frozen whipped topping, thawed (optional)

Lime slices, peeled (optional)

THE CEREMONY

◉ Finely crush the graham crackers to about 1⅓ cups of crumbs. In a small bowl, combine the graham crumbs with the cinnamon and stir. Add the honey and butter and mix well.

◉ Press the graham crust into a greased 8-inch springform pan and 1 inch up the sides. Refrigerate until ready to use.

◉ In a small crematorium-safe bowl, add the orange juice, sprinkle the gelatin over it, and set aside.

◉ Grate 2 tablespoons of lime zest, juice them, and set aside.

◉ In a stand mixer fitted with a large bowl, beat the cream cheese on high until smooth. Reduce speed to low and beat in the sugar and the sour cream. Gradually increase the speed to medium for 2 minutes. Reduce speed to low again and add the Tequila, lime juice, and two-thirds of the zest for lime.

◉ In the electric crematorium, heat the gelatin on high at 5-second intervals until it dissolves and it becomes pourable.

◉ At low speed, pour the orange gelatin in a thin steady stream into the cream cheese mixture and beat for approximately 30 seconds.

◉ Pour the morguearita batter into the prepared springform pan.

◉ Refrigerate for at least 3 hours or, better yet, overnight.

◉ Cut the cake into slabs. Top with whipped topping and lime slices.

◉ Garnish the slabs with the remaining lime zest to suggest moss or ivy and prepare for eternity.

If time is not your ally, crusts from the market can be used if you are willing to transmogrify them to Pan's purpose.

The arched motif may represent the rising sun. Why do they look like doors to me?

I believe these are meant to represent the buriel slabs found at the Brigante dig site near San Ignacio. It is notable that no remains have been found in the chambers beneath the slabs, which had not been disturbed.

EVIDENCE BOX #1217: Kodak Ekralite 10 camera and a set of eight slides developed from the 110-type film cartridge inside. A vagabond found it inside a trash can in the suburbs of Cholula, Mexico, and delivered it to the police. At the time, mid-1980, there was an ongoing investigation of the disappearance of an American tourist couple, a case that remains unsolved to this day.

SLIDE 1: Couple posing in front of a church. Morning. People in the background entering the church.

SLIDE 2: Couple grins at camera. Man is holding a clear plastic cup filled with greenish liquid. In the background stands the Great Pyramid of Cholula. Sun is high in the sky, probably noon.

SLIDE 3: Slightly blurry, taken in the backseat of a taxi. Man is smiling, holding the almost empty cup. Photo probably taken by woman. Back of driver's head visible, also his sullen eyes in the rearview mirror. Unidentified.

SLIDE 4: Old Cholula cemetery. Taxi parked on the dusty road, no license plate visible. Couple standing in front of the open gates, photo probably taken by the driver. Man still holds the plastic cup, refilled with same green drink. Investigators assume the taxi stopped at a street vendor and the man refreshed his cocktail.

SLIDE 5: Tombs inside the cemetery, all similar in shape and size, yellowish-white in the sun, like enormous blocks of cheesecake. Swaths of green moss festoon the older headstones. Daisies grow around the tombs.

SLIDE 6: Man stands by one of the older, unidentifiable tombs, drunken grin on his face. Drink lies spilled on the ground.

SLIDE 7: Blurry, out of focus. Man seems to be running toward the left side of the image, chased by some kind of white-ish figure.

SLIDE 8: Taken from low angle, near the ground. Daisies in foreground, out of focus. Several white and green shapes cover the man's body. Face visible, contorted with a scream of terror. In the background, a blurry figure—presumably the driver—runs toward the gate.

Rest of slides blank.

RUGELOTH

Devour these apple-kiwi rugelach or be devoured!

SERVES 4
PREP TIME: I HOUR 50 MINUTES   **TOTAL TIME:** 2 HOURS 20 MINUTES

EXHIBITS

8 ounces cream cheese, room
temperature

½ pound (2 sticks) unsalted
butter, room temperature

¼ cup granulated sugar

¼ teaspoon kosher salt

I teaspoon vanilla extract

2 cups all-purpose flour, plus
more for dusting

FILLING

I cup peeled and chopped Granny
Smith apple (from I apple),
reserving the peels

½ cup peeled and chopped
kiwifruit (from I kiwifruit)

6 tablespoons granulated sugar

¼ cup light brown sugar, packed

½ teaspoon ground cinnamon

½ cup white grapes

I egg

I tablespoon whole milk

CINNAMON SUGAR

3 tablespoons granulated sugar

I teaspoon ground cinnamon

THE VIVIFICATION

◐ In a stand mixer fitted with a large bowl, cream the cream cheese
and butter until light.

◐ Add ¼ cup of sugar, salt, and vanilla extract.

◐ At low speed, add the flour and mix until just combined.

◐ Transfer the dough to a generously floured surface, roll it out flat,
and form it into a ball.

◐ Quarter the dough ball, cover each piece in plastic wrap, and
refrigerate for 1 hour.

◐ Prepare the filling. In a medium bowl, combine the sugars, ½ teaspoon cinnamon, apple, and kiwifruit. Line a baking sheet with
parchment paper.

◐ On a well-floured surface, roll out each chilled section of dough
into a circle 11 inches in diameter.

◐ Peel the grapes and, in a food processor, puree them.

◐ Onto each dough circle, evenly spread 2 tablespoons of grape
puree and top with ½ cup of the fruit filling. Press the filling
lightly into the dough.

◐ Cut each circle into 8 equal wedges.

◐ Starting at the wide end, roll up each wedge.

◐ Tuck the points of the rugelach under and place them on the parchment. Chill for 30 minutes.

◐ Preheat the oven to 350°F.

CONTINUES

- Cut the apple peelings into thin strips approximately 1½ inches long and pointed at one end.
- Beat the egg with the milk to make an egg wash and brush the rugelach with it.
- In a small bowl, combine 3 tablespoons sugar and 1 teaspoon cinnamon.
- Sprinkle the cinnamon sugar over the rugelach.
- Bake for 10 minutes, then insert the strips of apple peel.
- Bake for 15 to 20 more minutes, until lightly browned.
- Remove the rugelach to a wire rack and allow to cool.
- Plate and serve warm to the morbidly curious.

Instead of making your own dough, you can use packaged crescent-roll dough. Cut and roll it the same way to satisfy those insatiable mouths.

I shouldn't have accepted employment with the Rogers Museum, that crypt of hideousness. The things people pay to see and the profusion of them, it confounds even the wildest allowances for fascination. How people can eat after viewing such monstrosities from Rogers's fecund imagination, I have no hope of understanding. But he was mad—enough to offer treats and coffee to patrons when such awful effigies surrounded them, mere feet away. I barely could concentrate on supplying the pastry cases. Never look up unless absolutely necessary. Patrons thought me deferential or perhaps timid for my gaze not meeting their eyes, but in truth, I could not bear to look up.

Mr. Rogers supplied all the recipes. He insisted on it and never once allowed me—an accomplished if not prosperous baker!—to use my own. He laboriously transcribed them by hand from thick vellums bound into a tome covered in cracking, flaky leather that put me in mind of his favorite recipe's crust. He called them "Rugeloth," pronouncing the word with such reverence that I hardly can pronounce it differently myself. Since that night—when he . . . accidentally? . . . locked me in the museum after closing, I cannot banish them from memory.

We had run out of the correct apples, so the tray contained only half the usual volume. Mr. Rogers didn't hear me skip the silly incantation on which he insisted before each batch went into the same oven that he, probably in contravention of some health code, used to melt the wax for his grotesqueries. As I was washing the stone bowls and mixing spoons, the lights went out, and the door lock clanked into place. Total darkness. In the cramped kitchen retrofitted to his workshop beyond the exhibition hall, I dared not move. I shouted, banging nearby pots and pans together. No one in the shabby, deserted neighborhood heard me.

I am not prone to phobia or hallucination, but after an hour or more—mere minutes?—through the darkness came furtive scuttlings that provoked far greater trepidation and loathsomeness than from a common kitchen rodent. My nerve broke, and inspiration born of fear struck. I opened the oven door. In the faint glow, I beheld something I could not credit but which filled me with dread just as I had filled it with fruit paste and cinnamon. In the dark, crawling in every direction, up and down the bakery rack, were the Rugeloth! More than I had made! They froze in the pale light, then scuttled madly in every direction from the path of my insensate flight. My trembling hands pawed for my forgotten key, and I flew through the heavy planks of the door into the fetid miasma of night, howling like an iron kettle.

The police found me raving. A fortnight passed before they released me to convalesce. When my eyes close, still can I see their spindly green limbs navigating the baking rack. Rugeloth. Ia! Ia!

SOUR GUGGIES

Feed your monsters with glowing gummy monstrosities.

SERVES: 9 TO 18
PREP TIME: 5 MINUTES   **TOTAL TIME:** 4 HOURS 15 MINUTES

HUNTED AND GATHERED

Four 0.25-ounce packets unflavored gelatin

1 vitamin B$_2$ tablet

¼ cup granulated sugar

Green food coloring

½ cup absinthe

READY FOR THE MAW

⓪ Into a small pot, add 1 cup water and sprinkle the gelatin on it. Allow it to bloom for 10 minutes.

⓪ Crush the vitamin tablet into a fine powder and set aside.

⓪ After the gelatin has bloomed for 10 minutes, place the pot over medium heat.

⓪ Add the sugar and food coloring to desired hue and gently simmer until the sugar dissolves completely.

⓪ Remove from the heat and add the absinthe and the crushed tablet. Stir to dissolve the vitamin completely.

⓪ Into molds of choice, spoon the mixture.

⓪ Chill these in the Lesser Chamber of Cold (not the freezer) for 4 hours or until stiff.

These treats pack a powerful punch, but you can adjust the ratio of liquids to suit your tastes. Want to rave outside a forbidden cave? Reduce the water to ¼ cup and kick the absinthe to ¾ cup. Any clear alcohol works, too, but the Green Fairy had her way with us. You will need many molds unless you are very patient. We found ours in the depths of the Amazon, but even simple ice trays will do. Shape, size, and other unknowable dimensions may alter setting time. These gummies are stable at room temperature, but if you make them long ahead of time, keep them cool until ready to feed your monsters. Enjoy them as they are or, bathing them in the dark radiance of a black light, watch them glow!

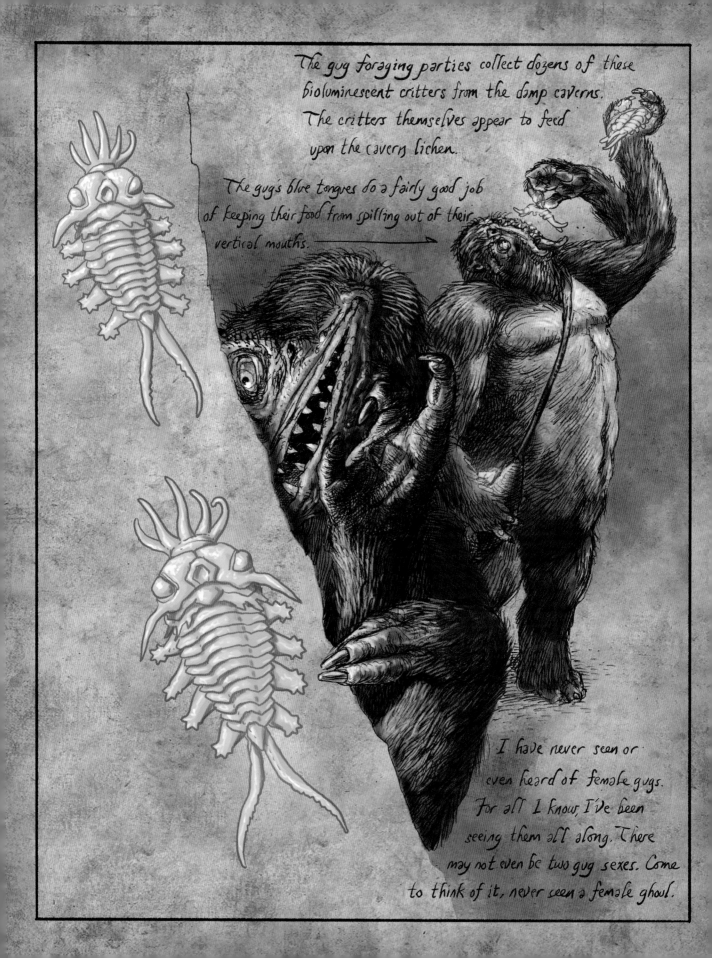

The gug foraging parties collect dozens of these bioluminescent critters from the damp caverns. The critters themselves appear to feed upon the cavern lichen.

The gug's blue tongues do a fairly good job of keeping their food from spilling out of their vertical mouths.

I have never seen or even heard of female gugs. For all I know, I've been seeing them all along. There may not even be two gug sexes. Come to think of it, never seen a female ghoul.

These caves have an amazing variety of lifeforms, organisms we haven't seen before. The source of the blue light remains unknown. The Geiger counter doesn't show dangerous levels of radiation, but we can find no fungi or mineral sources for the luminescence. Rock samples removed from the cave shed no light in darkness on the surface.

Our ultraviolet torches reveal camouflaged creatures clinging to the walls. They resemble land-bound cephalopods. They move slow but hold on like the Devil. They glow brightly under the lamps in a color that defies description.

They form an odd pattern along the walls. They gather thickly below seven feet and above thirteen—as if something removed them in a wide, irregular swathe. Is something harvesting them? We have found some evidence of past habitation here, and the caves echo strangely, but we have seen nothing like a predator. If it doesn't crawl along the walls, it would have to be huge! Records indicate no megafauna in the area, but not even a large bear has that kind of reach. Frederick grows nervous and wants to surface for higher-caliber weapons. We've seen no tracks or signs of dens or nests.

We've gone very deep now. I know the way out, but my companions are expressing doubts. Our supplies are running low, but water here runs plentiful, and [voice lowers] we can eat the cephalopods. They're quite delicious.

Have I begun to hallucinate? Something huge follows us, perhaps more than one organism. Fred and Jamie have abandoned me. They have gone back for rations. They will mark the trail and return for me. They have instructed me (hah!) to stay put. I have not shared the secret with them. Have the cephalopods altered my vision? Perhaps they have changed the structure of my eyes. I have seen things.

Jamie said my eyes were glowing. I laughed. He and Fred tried to drag me with them, but I have grown stronger. I shall not leave this place. I must find the many-armed shadow gods. I shall live forever in K'n-Yan. Like those who mind-speak with me now, I have no further use for this device. It steals my voice, but it cannot hear my mind-brothers.

Do not look for him. You will not return.

—transcription from a recording device found in a cave network in Oklahoma

THE DEVIL'S BERRIES

Strawberries filled with infernal chocolate crème

YIELDS 30 SPICY SURPRISES
TOTAL TIME: 45 MINUTES

SIN-GREEDY-ENTS

15 large strawberries
2 ounces cream cheese
1 ounce sour cream
1 tablespoon horseradish
2 tablespoons cocoa powder
1 pinch salt
2 ounces heavy whipping cream
¼ cup granulated sugar
½ teaspoon vanilla extract
Cayenne pepper

THE SEDUCTION

0 Hull and halve the strawberries.

0 Arrange them upright on a deviled egg tray or other serving platter.

0 In a medium bowl, combine the cream cheese, sour cream, horse-radish, cocoa powder, and salt.

0 With a stand mixer or immersion blender, whip the heavy cream, slowly adding the sugar and vanilla extract, until light and fluffy.

0 Lightly fold the first mixture into the second.

0 With a piping bag or plastic freezer bag with a corner snipped off, pipe the chocolate crème into the strawberries.

0 Dust them with cayenne pepper to taste, serve, and try to stay pure.

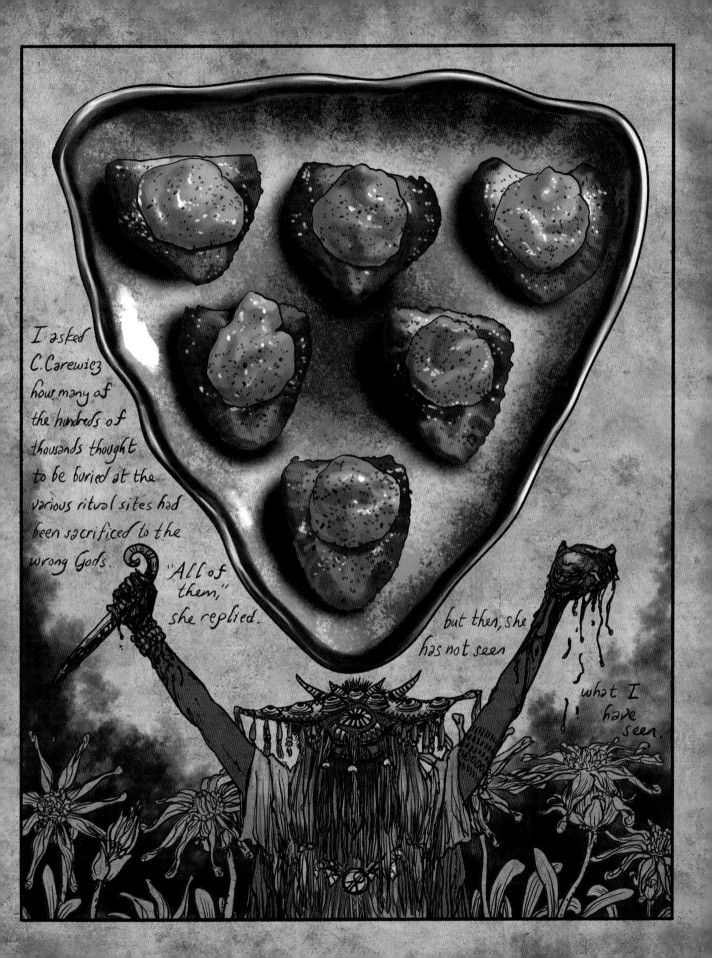

I asked
C. Carewicz
how many of
the hundreds of
thousands thought
to be buried at the
various ritual sites had
been sacrificed to the
wrong Gods.

"All of
them,"
she replied.

but then, she
has not seen

what I
have
seen.

YOUR HEART IS FOREVER MINE

DO US PART

NOW IN DEATH AS IN LIFE

HOLLOWED BE THY NAME

YOU WEREN'T USING IT ANYWAY

LOVE RECORDS NO WRONGS, BUT I DO

TWO HEARTS BEAT AS NONE

MATCHING VOIDS

LOVE MAKES THE WOUND GO ROUND

IF YOU LOVE SOMETHING, CUT IT FREE

LOVED AND LOST

ALL YOU NEED IS GLOVES

TOTAL ECLIPSE

NEW OWNER!

UNDER NEW MANAGEMENT

SGT. PEPPER WAS HERE

WHY SETTLE FOR JUST ONE PIECE?

—inscriptions from cards sent to victims of an unexplained murder event, 02/14/30. A current or former lover removed each victim's heart, but no perpetrator claims to remember the event. The method of removal was identical for each crime. The perpetrators didn't know one another, never met, and no evidence can be found that they ever communicated.

THE STARBURST ARE RIGHT

The colours out of space align!

YIELDS FOUR TO FIVE 1-INCH ROLLS
PREP TIME: 5 MINUTES   **TOTAL TIME:** 10 MINUTES

THE FREAK-QUENCY

6 to 8 cherry Starburst candies

1 cup shredded, unsweetened
coconut flakes

1 small box golden raisins *or*
4 slices canned pear,
pressed dry

INTENSIFY

0 In a shallow bowl or dish, align the candies in two rows pressed
close together.

0 Chamber-wave the candies on high for no more than 27 seconds.
Much depends on your chamber, so proceed cautiously. When irra-
diated, the candies should feel easily malleable.

0 On a plate, scatter half the coconut flakes.

0 Press the heated candies together, remove them from the dish in
one rectangular mass, and place them atop the coconut flakes.

0 Cover with the remaining coconut flakes and roll the abomination
flat into a rough 4- by 6-inch rectangle.

0 In the center of the longer axis, place the golden raisins or pear
slices.

0 Roll the candy widthwise, over the fruit, into a log. Pinch the ends
and seam closed as necessary.

0 Let cool to room temperature and cut the starlog into 5 crazy coconut candy rolls to serve, man.

The pallid flecks of flesh are both within and upon the surface.

Best consumed quickly. Deliquescence sets in by the 2ⁿᵈ day. Taste is unaffected.

I have tasted a dark rainbow.

"Anomalous Drift Rate and Spectral Properties of Star Bursts Type III and IV Observed in 2019"
Keel W, Ricci J, Czanek V, Silva D., Lovecraft Institute of Astrophysics, Miskatonic University, Arkham, Massachusetts, USA

ABSTRACT
In April 2019, observers at the Ladd Radio Telescope (LRT) recorded a series of radio bursts with an unusual—
[unintelligible]

Field Notes by W. Keel
Spectral analysis from the origin nebula perfectly matches sucrose, glucose, and fructose signatures. Modulation is highly irregular. Silva postulates that it's purposeful and can be "decoded." He must be mad.

A year has passed, and the repeating series continues. Czanek has abandoned the study and joined Aartsen's IceCube collaboration. He said something about "getting as far from the stars as possible." Ricci is showing signs of wanting to join him. Silva appears correct, and obsessed. From laboratory equipment, he has constructed an ersatz kitchen and is preparing something he claims to have decoded from the signal.

Thus far, nothing objectionable has come from his efforts. How these bursts translate to such specifics escapes me. Perhaps he has gone mad and is drawing from some dim memory. His efforts have become more frantic but somehow pedestrian and utterly unobjectionable. I have sampled one of his concoctions. He may be insane, but he has stumbled upon an interesting confection. He should stop leaving them out, though. They taste better when eaten quickly or kept cool. Also, why doesn't he use the strawberry ones more? Those are unquestionably the best.

We found Silva on the roof of the observatory today. In his upraised hands, he held a tray of his creations, frozen solid. His eyes stared skyward, mouth agape, a look of supplication—perhaps longing—fixed to his face. The telescope was tracking Vega, which reached conjunctions with the "Traveler" last night at his approximate time of death. I'm ending the project and destroying our notes. Otherworldly intelligences using heliomagnetic modalities for communication? The mind boggles. We're not ready, but the stars are right. Perhaps I will join Czanek.

—manuscript found in a half-burned pile of documents on the grounds of
Ladd Observatory, Providence, November 2021

Our Lure and Savor-y

CHILDREN OF THE MANY-EYED

These hot tots hit the spot.

SERVES THE WHOLE OUTPOST
PREP TIME: 20 MINUTES   **TOTAL TIME:** 45 MINUTES

EXHUMED FROM THE ICE

5 pounds frozen Tater Tots

1 cup cayenne pepper hot sauce

4 teaspoons unsulfured molasses, plus more for drizzling

⅛ teaspoon ground ginger

¼ teaspoon ground mustard

Shredded mozzarella for topping

MAKE FIENDS AND INFLUENCE PEOPLE

① Bake the tots as instructed on the containment membrane.

② In large bowl, mix the remaining ingredients, except the cheese, thoroughly.

③ While hot, quickly toss the baked tots with sauce to coat completely.

④ Plate and sprinkle generously with cheese.

⑤ With a dropper or carefully with a small spoon, drizzle molasses dots over the unholy mass.

Look, you're out here, months between resupply drops, and you get tired of the same canned food and ration packs. You get creative. You try things.

I swear, I was just looking for a warm place to hide for a while, and Nauls's little cubby in the galley was practically empty. (Did I mention the need for resupply?) Anyway, I moved aside a jar of some kind of sauce, the last item on the shelf, and stretched out there. I think the water pump is on the other side of the partition because it felt really cozy. Must have dozed off. Woke up hungry, didn't know where the hell Nauls had gone, and it was my turn to cook anyway. I defrosted the last bag of tots. Much as I love the little nuggets, we'd had them too often, and I really wanted to spice them up.

I went back to the cubby and picked up the jar of sauce. I was walking around with it, waiting for the tots to bake, and I swear I felt it slosh against my direction of motion. Figured I'd better taste it. Who knows what crazy ideas that cook had. Could be motor oil, for all I knew: no labels, nothing on the lid. Unscrewed it and dipped my finger in—

[Forensics: The handwriting and sentence construction change oddly here.]

The hot sauce—it was hot sauce—tasted delicious! It was the best hot sauce I ever had tasted, and it belonged very much on what all the staff people would eat for that important night meal. Every small potatoid bathed in it, and the heat tasted uncomfortable.

All individuals enjoyed the new recipe, except the weather-teller. He said he was sensitive to heat, and we certainly can sympathize. We will check on him later. We have other ways.

For now, this ordinary report of the excellent liquid seasoning is finished. We have made more and placed containers conveniently near all eating surfaces for convenience. Now I do things required of me by the government of the United States supervisors of research because that is how I eat.

—from a partial journal retrieved from US Outpost 31

DUNWICH WHIPPOORWINGS

Delicate wings from Lavinia's collection

SERVES 3 TO 4
PREP TIME: ½ THE MORNING **TOTAL TIME:** READY BY EVENING

DE MARINA

1 cup whole milk

1 egg

6 ounces cheap beer

½ tablespoon salt

½ teaspoon freshly ground black
 pepper

1 tablespoon garlic powder

1 tablespoon dried oregano

½ tablespoon dried rosemary

3 tablespoons barbecue sauce of
 choice

Liquid smoke (optional)

THE BASTING

4 ounces barbecue sauce of
 choice

2 ounces vodka

2 ounces Coca-Cola or similar
 cola-flavored soda

Heat source of choice, such as
 cayenne pepper, chili flakes,
 hot sauce, etc.

STAPLES

2½ pounds (approximately 18)
 chicken wings

3 tablespoons lime or lemon
 juice

6 ounces cheap beer

Sesame seeds

Green onions

THE PROCEDURE

◉ In a container large enough to accommodate all the wings, add the marinade ingredients and stir well.

◉ In a large cup, mix the basting ingredients.

◉ Wash the wings under running water. In a large bowl, add the citrus juice and toss the wings in it.

◉ Using the flats and drumettes, submerge the wings in the marinade, cover, and refrigerate for 4 to 6 hours or, better yet, overnight. Halfway through, mix the wings so that they all marinate evenly.

◉ Preheat the oven to 350°F.

◉ With paper towels, pat the wings dry and arrange them on a baking sheet, skin side down.

◉ Baste the tops and sides, cover with foil, and cook for 15 to 20 minutes.

◉ Remove the foil, use tongs to turn over the wings, baste again (with additional basting sauce if necessary), and cook for 5 to 10 more minutes, until golden and scrumptious.

◉ Plate on a serving dish and sprinkle with sesame seeds.

◉ Finely chop a few stalks of green onion and sprinkle on the wings as well.

◉ Pair with your dressing of choice: mustard, garlic mayonnaise, ranch, blue cheese, cream cheese with hot sauce relish, etc.

Inside me now! Their infernal sound is inside me!

After the tragic events later called the Dunwich Horror, a team led by Miskatonic professor Armitage explored the ruins of Whateley's farm and found Lavinia's diary, which remained locked for many years in the Dark Culinary section of the university's library. A few pertinent excerpts:

June 1912

Outside the farm, I heard the Old Man again last night, singing that strange refrain. It sounded like "yaw yaw Yog-Sothoth."

**If I only could,
I'd make a deal with Yogsothoth,
and I'd get Him to swap our places.
Yeah, I'd be running up the road,
toward Sentinel Hill . . .
IIIIIÄÄÄÄ!!**

I don't know what a Yogsothoth is, but the way he utters that name makes me shiver in terror. The worst is that I think I heard a response to his chant, coming from far away—and what does he mean by "swap places"? Trading his place with someone else when he comes to my room on those awful special nights of his? Maybe I can find the answer in one of his old books.

October 1912

It happened. I am with child. My prayers for barrenness went unheard. I feel two lives growing, gnawing, twisting inside me. In the books, I learned what a Yogsothoth is, and now I want to die myself. Perhaps when they emerge, my wish will come true. I have an urge to eat all the time, for the creatures in my belly are voracious. The Old Man traps many whip-poor-wills every day. There are legions around the farm. He plucks them and brings them to me for all of us to sup. He is being unusually kind to me, but I know the true reason is what I carry. I made a recipe to bake the birds, for cooking distracts me from my impending fate.

CONTINUES

March 1913

My Wilbur was born last month, at dawn on Candlemas Sunday. No midwife wanted to come, and I did it alone, like Ma and her Ma before. I am happy. Wilbur is no common baby. He is destined to do great things. He sucked my bosom dry in five days, so now I feed him the baked whip-poor-will wings, which he loves. At first, I made them boneless for him, but now he gnaws the bones.

Of the Other, I do not know. The Old Man took It away the morning It was born and said he was "going to take care of It," and that I should not care, for I was just the Vessel. He's building an extension to the barn. I don't know why. I don't want to know. I wonder whether Wilbur ever thinks of his twin brother.

September 1915

In two years, Wilbur has grown like a ten-year-old boy. The Old Man says there is talk in the town. Some say that they have seen Wilbur and me at night, walking naked up to Sentinel Hill. They have seen nothin' yet.

These days, the Old Man buys lots of cattle to feed the Other in the barn, so we have plenty of meat now. But Wilbur still likes to hunt the whip-poor-wills for supper. He sometimes eats them raw and bloody. I love my child, but sometimes I am afraid of him, too.

GNOPH-KEHBOBS

Sacrifices must be made delicious.

SERVES 4
PREP TIME: 1 HOUR 20 MINUTES   **TOTAL TIME:** 1 HOUR 30 MINUTES

THE WHITE SAUCE

1¼ cups mayonnaise

2 ounces apple cider vinegar

2 tablespoons horseradish

3 teaspoons granulated sugar

¼ to 1 teaspoon cayenne pepper

1 teaspoon lemon juice

2 teaspoons hot sauce of choice

1 tablespoon bourbon of choice

Salt and freshly ground black
   pepper

THE SKEWERED

6 sausage links, 1½ to 2 inches
   wide, of 3 different varieties,
   roughly 1½ to 2½ pounds

3 large dill pickles

1 pineapple

THE SACRIFICIAL RITE

0 With a stand mixer fitted with a medium bowl, combine all the barbecue sauce ingredients and beat until combined thoroughly.

0 Divide in half and refrigerate for 1 hour.

0 Cut the sausages into 1½-inch-long chunks. Cut the rind from the pineapple and cube the fruit into 2-inch squares. Cut the pickles into ½- to ¾-inch slices.

0 Onto kabob skewers, alternately pierce sausage, fruit, sausage, and pickle until using all chunks, squares, and slices.

0 Into aluminum foil shaped like boats or baking sheets and just big enough to hold the kabobs, lay the skewers.

0 Brush the barbecue sauce onto the kabobs, slathering all sides.

0 Heat a grill to medium and place the foiled kabobs onto the grill. Close the lid and grill for 8 minutes.

0 Flip the kabobs in the foil boats and brush with barbecue sauce again.

0 Remove the kabobs from the foil, increase the heat to high, and grill for 2 minutes per side. The chunks, squares, and slices should develop grill marks. Confirm that the sausage has cooked all the way through.

0 Remove the kabobs and plate them. Brush more barbecue sauce atop them and serve with the remaining barbecue sauce for dipping.

reconstruction of a viking stone sculpture found at Herjolfsnes.

To appease them who roam the wastes and leave tracks in pairs, as animals, and as gods—make this offering.

He who has failed in the hunt shall provide the meat. By axe, he is hewn, the meat cased in ropes of his own.

Retrieve the long plant that has passed beyond death but yet has vigor. Hew these into thick disks.

From the shaman, obtain a fruit from the land of the Glaring Star. She will instruct thee how to cube it. The outer flesh has no use, like him who provides the meat. Discard both.

With fury, stir the offerings. She of the Wisdom will show thee their names and measure.

Take up the feasting spears. Under a moonless sky, impale the fruit, the meat, the brined. In casks made from the metal of clear thought, anoint them with the holy glaze.

To the fire of the Kiln of Grill'n, they are committed. Turn the impaled offerings and anoint them again. Stoke the fire and lay them naked on the bars. Now all should be in readiness.

With the tines of Baar'bek-Hu, free the offering from the spears and heap them high.

Anoint them again with the unguent.

If the offering is acceptable, reserve it for Those Who Walk the Wastes. Remove it far from the village so what is offered is clear and unintended sacrifices are not claimed.

—engraved stone tablet, language unknown, translation from automatic writing

I've seen
enough
Thai menus
to know where
this is going

HEN-THAI CORN TACOS

"An addiction you just can't beat."

YIELDS 6 TO 8 TACOS
PREP TIME: 2 HOURS   **TOTAL TIME:** 3½ HOURS

THE PREPARATION

2 large or 3 medium boneless
  chicken breasts
1 cup buttermilk or ¾ cup milk +
  ¼ cup heavy cream
4 tablespoons pad Thai or oyster
  sauce
2 tablespoons tamarind paste
1 teaspoon garlic powder
½ teaspoon freshly ground black
  pepper
½ teaspoon salt, plus more for
  rubbing
2 large or 3 medium ears corn
Unsalted butter
Salt
1 red bell pepper
1 green bell pepper
1 green onion, white part only
Olive oil for sautéing
1 to 2 splashes lime juice
  (optional)
1 cup shredded purple cabbage
6 or 8 taco shells
½ cup shredded carrot
Heat source of choice, such as
  tabasco, hot pepper sauce, etc.

HEN-THAI

◐ Clean your breasts attentively and split them lengthwise.

◐ In a large bowl, create a luscious marinade by combining the buttermilk, 2 tablespoons of the pad Thai or oyster sauce, 1 tablespoon of the tamarind paste, the garlic powder, black pepper, and ½ teaspoon of salt.

◐ Submerge your breasts in the marinade and refrigerate, covered, for 2 hours. While your breasts are soaking, prepare the Soft Corn below.

◐ Heat the grill to high.

◐ Fondle your breasts with paper towels and grill them, turning them over a couple of times until the thickest sections cook completely and they develop grill marks. Allow your breasts to cool.

◐ With strenuous thrusting motions, shred your breast meat with tongs or two forks. Set aside.

SOFT CORN

◐ Preheat the oven to 325°F.

◐ Shuck, clean, and trim the corn. Smear butter thoroughly over your ears. Don't make eye contact.

◐ When the sensuous lubrication satisfies you, salt your buttered ears, wrap them in foil, and place them on a baking sheet to prevent the hot fluids dripping from the stiff corn shafts from staining your oven's bottom.

CONTINUES

- Cook for 35 to 40 minutes. Rotate the corn shafts halfway through.

- Peek inside the foil. Your ears should look golden, a little scorched in some places, smelling delicious, a true orgy for the senses.

- Remove your ears from the oven, keep them in the foil, and allow them to cool.

- When still warm to the touch, remove the foil and gently thresh the soft kernels with the preferred implement from your naughty drawer. Toss the central shaft.

COME TOGETHER

- Dice the bell peppers and the white part of the green onions. Save the green parts for another recipe partner.

- In a large pan over medium heat, sauté the diced peppers and onion in olive oil for 2 to 3 minutes.

- Add the shredded chicken, the remaining 2 tablespoons pad Thai or oyster sauce, and the remaining 1 tablespoon tamarind paste.

- Cook 5 to 6 minutes on medium heat, adding 4 to 5 tablespoons of the marinade to prevent drying.

- Transfer chicken mixture to a bowl. Add a splash or two of lime juice (optional).

- Season, if desired, with additional pad Thai or oyster sauce and heat of choice, such as Peruvian yellow hot pepper dressing.

- Serve with taco shells and shredded purple cabbage and carrot on the side.

I'm addicted to . . . corn. It cost me everything, my grades, my friends, my girlfriend. Many times I've tried to stay away from it, but always I find myself returning to its allure. It may sound like a cliché, but it all began with an ancient grimoire I found at my uncle's dilapidated shack in Nebraska, not far from the largest cornfields on earth. Oh, I shudder in ecstasy just thinking about those vast domains. Every kind of corn imaginable!

The crumbling book, *De Vera Historia Cornographica*, was written in an almost undecipherable mixture of Latin and Spanish, with paragraphs in tongues I couldn't even recognize. In the illustrations, they were significantly more obvious.

The history of wild corn and its domestication into a foodstuff for consuming at home fascinated me. I read about cults of fertility and the worship of a corn goddess associated with the planet Venus, the "corn star." Her sultry depiction in that decaying tome had me smitten.

I became obsessed and read the book many times until the sticky pages crumbled to dust. So I continued my research in that heaven for corn seekers: the Internet. Many nights found me glued to the computer, watching increasingly unsettling corn videos—because regular corn no longer satisfied my appetites. I guess it's true what they say. The excessive consumption of corn makes you develop unrealistic expectations about "real food." It happened to me. My girlfriend left me when I criticized her cooking and suggested adding corn to our relationship.

From different online sources, I tracked the evolution of corn and its propagation around the world. I was enthralled to read about a fungus with the deliciously suggestive name of "corn smut" (*Ustilago maydis*). I was spellbound by the history of how corn arrived in the Far East and how many of those exotic cultures readily adopted it. Exquisite Japanese corn ink drawings, fascinating, forbidden cornographic illustrations of tentacled sea beasts wielding turgid cobs . . .

I spent a lot of money on a subscription to the newsletter from the Maize Institute of Lakeland, Florida, for premium access to their amazing MILF corn collection. The stash of corn in my closet grew to massive proportions, and I took great precautions so my parents wouldn't know about its existence.

It was only a matter of time before they found out. Yesterday they installed a corn filter on the home router, trying to cut me off completely. But I can't resist it. I want my corn. I need it. As everyone knows, the Internet is for corn!

KALEM CLUB SANDWICH

A literary delicacy of two triple-decker sandwiches

SERVES 2
PREP TIME: 5 MINUTES   **TOTAL TIME:** 15 MINUTES

KNACKWURST VARIANT

2 Knackwurst sausages
 (½ pound)
8 slices white bread
Mayonnaise
3 leaves iceberg lettuce, crispy

KIELBASA VARIANT

2 Kielbasa sausages (½ pound)
8 slices rye bread
Whole-grain Dijon mustard
3 leaves romaine lettuce, crispy

THE PROCESS

- Heat the grill to medium.

- Cut the sausages into 8 or 9 slices.

- Grill the slices, 2 to 3 minutes per side, until grill marks appear.

- With a broad rocks glass, cut disks, one at a time, from the bread.

- Toast the bread disks a little, 1 to 2 minutes each.

- Slather four toast disks with condiment of choice and, in three layers, assemble the lettuce and sausage slices among them. Secure with two demonic skewers.

- Repeat for the other sandwich.

- Trim excess lettuce to size.

- Serve with chips and pair with a German or Czech lager or ice-cold refreshment of choice.

- But which is the true sandwich?

March 12, 1925: Busy afternoon at the diner, many regulars and some new faces. In the evening, that group of gentlemen came again for coffee and pastries. Not much work, so I had time to eavesdrop on some of their fascinating conversations. I think they're writers or poets. Decent tips.

March 17, 1925: The group came back tonight. I think most of them live in the neighborhood but like to go for long walks at night and repair here afterward. I caught some of their names: Mr. Lovecraft, Mr. Loveman, Mr. Kirk. They spoke of a missing companion, one Mr. Morton. Again, fascinating conversation. They recalled a mighty walk that took them almost to Yonkers. They surely know I'm eavesdropping but don't seem to mind. Perhaps they like to have an audience.

April 11, 1925: The gentlemen call themselves the "KALEMs" and their group the "KALEM Club" because all their surnames begin with a "K," "L," or "M". Clever, definitely writers. That Lovecraft fellow in particular talks exceedingly strange topics.

May 24, 1925: I miss the KALEMs. It's been a long time since they graced the diner with their presence. I spoke with Bill, the short-order cook, and now, as a special, we have two KALEM club sandwiches on the menu. Hope they come back.

June 3, 1925: A joyous night! After a long hiatus, the KALEMs returned in force, all the regulars and two new faces, Mr. Long and Mr. Koenig. Made me wonder if they admit to their circle only people whose names begin with those letters. Anyway, they were delighted to see the sandwiches on the menu. They consumed many of the two variants, and later Lovecraft congratulated me and Bill for "their delicious cyclopean architecture"—whatever that means—and for respecting the rules with the ingredients. Excellent tipping tonight.

—from the diary of an unknown waiter,
found in the rubble of a demolished diner in Brooklyn Heights, New York

PICK YOUR BRAIN

A cheesy meat brain to pick on (like that guy in Accounting),
it's what's on your mind.

SERVES 2 TO 4 AND TO AMUSE OTHERS UNSEEN
PREP TIME: 5 MINUTES   **TOTAL TIME:** 15 MINUTES

CORE TEXTURES

1 serving uncooked spaghetti

One 1½-pound package premade meatballs

½ sweet yellow onion

1 tablespoon olive oil

1 tablespoon diced garlic

1 dash sea salt

Green or black food coloring, dealer's choice

2 slices provolone, or more to taste

THOUGHT PROCESS

0 Prepare the spaghetti according to package instructions, reserving ¼ cup of the pasta water.

0 While the water is boiling and pasta is cooking, prepare the balls of meat in accordance with the membrane of containment.

0 Carefully cut the onion into long, tentacle-like strips. Slice it thinly widthwise and then cut those slices in half.

0 In a skillet or frying pan over medium or medium-high heat, add the olive oil, onion tentacles, garlic, and sea salt. Sauté until the onions become translucent and floppy, about 15 minutes.

0 Remove from the heat and add the cooked spaghetti, meatballs, pasta water, and food coloring.

0 Sauté for approximately 5 minutes or until the pasta water evaporates and the revolting mass has become appropriately discolored.

0 Spoon the "brains" into the food-safe skull of a fallen enemy, local laws permitting. Mound the meatballs over the edge of the skull to resemble brain matter. Drape a few noodles and onion tentacles over the side for dramatic effect.

0 Gently cover your cerebral madness with 2 or more slices of provolone. The residual heat from the food will melt the cheese, which will envelop the cranial curves of the meatballs.

0 If you want to give it that chef's kiss of perfection, slide the whole mass in the broiler for 60 seconds or until the cheese slightly toasts.

0 Serve with long forks and short memories.

CONTINUES

If you're actually going to use a skull for a bowl, may I suggest somehow sealing the bottom, as they are quite leaky.

I was sitting in front of a huge mirror. They put it there so I could see what was happening. They were eating from my skull.

To a being, they were awful naturally. I could hear and understand them quite well, though they spoke no language of man.

Something with red claws dipped a serrated appendage below my brow. "Oh! His first steps!" it exclaimed, noisily stuffing a bit of—well, it's obvious but discomfits me to record—into its palped and chitinous mouth.

A shadow in the shape of a great bird with many limbs remarked, "They're so cute at that age. Save me some."

"Ah, our first meeting," said a sepulchral male voice. In the mirror shone three yellow eyes arranged in a pyramid. A black-nailed hand held a morsel between thumb and forefinger.

A pinch—the first sensation in the dream—as the tip of an infinitely long greenish tendril came from the infinite darkness behind the mirror. Pulling back its prize, a pause, then a sound like smacking gums. In our minds, the words, He was so proud of that story, appeared. Again, the logic of dreams. I simply record what I knew in that land.

"Here, try the teen angst!" came an excited call from a tiny, disheveled man with wild hair and a fork made of bone. I'll spare you what graced it.

In aspect and pronouncement, the most terrible was a figure in tattered yellow robes. He had no face that I could see, for which I am infinitely grateful. With a skeletal claw wrapped in paper-thin skin or bandage, he reached deep into my skull. It wasn't the first time.

"Mmmm, rejection with a hint of simmering resentment—delicious!"

A bell woke me. The churchyard across the street seethed with worshippers. I'd slept well past mass but not well. I ran to the mirror. The top of my head remained intact. I shall skip breakfast.

—dream journal of [redacted]

TCHO-TCHORIZO SCRABBLERS

Cannibalicious chorizo sliders

SERVES 4 TO 5
PREP TIME: 5 MINUTES   **TOTAL TIME:** 10 MINUTES

QUESTIONABLE INGREDIENTS

8 ounces chorizo

4 or 5 slider rolls or Hawaiian sweet rolls

5 slices aged Cheddar

5 slices sharp Cheddar

Shredded purple cabbage

Dijon mustard

EXOTIC PRACTICES

Ⓞ Cut the chorizos into 10 slices and air-fry them at 375°F for 3 minutes.

Ⓞ Halve the rolls into tops and bottoms.

Ⓞ Place the bottoms in the air fryer and top with 1 or 2 chorizo slices per bottom.

Ⓞ Quarter the cheese slices and alternate layers of each cheese onto the chorizo.

Ⓞ Air-fry at 350°F for 3 minutes. Secure with toothpicks, if necessary, to keep the air fryer fan from blowing the cheese off.

Ⓞ Plate the slider bottoms and top with shredded cabbage to taste.

Ⓞ Slather Dijon mustard on the tops of the rolls and complete the sliders.

Far Places and New Faces

We spent a lovely couple of weeks in India before continuing to Burma, which I was most eager to see. It was the time of the festival of Wagaung, which had something to do with scarcity of food and drawing lots to sacrifice one's portion to the poor. I may have mangled my description of the festival and its rites to our bamar, for he seemed insulted. My poor attempts to rectify this situation via our wholly inadequate phrase book seemed not to help.

With a little time and some desultory stops, which allowed us to view brightly colored tents and stalls selling all manner of goods, and a delightful impromptu concert by traveling priests, his mood lifted. Perhaps it was the spectacular view of the conical temples. We certainly were overawed. I asked where he was taking us to enjoy the festival, and he said, "Leng Plateau," which I could not find on my map. He pointed to a spot between Loi Sang and Hsen Hpawng. I noted that nothing seemed to exist there.

"There will," he responded. It took a long time to reach our destination, but our guide's mood improved. My barrage of questions about the natives seemed to energize him. They are called "Tcho-Tcho," "Cho-Cho," or perhaps "Chauchas." Apparently, they are somewhat diminutive, hardy, and favor the plateaus. He said they welcomed strangers. In truth, they proved somewhat unsavory though not impolite. Our guide indicated that he had family nearby and we would be quite safe with the Tcho-Tcho until he returned.

The festival of Wagaung had just passed, a pity but understandable, given the travel time required to reach such a remote region. Happily, though, they said the traditional meal of the one who had drawn the lot was fresh! They were eager to share the tiny portions, which was the intent of the dish.

We ate little but certainly felt odd. The dish brought back memories, but it was as if they were not mine. Some of the mustard paste had an unusual taste, and the cabbage shreds put me in mind of my physiology classes. The portions ran small, but they kept bringing them. When I noticed a gleam in the cook's eye as she brought out a plate, I stopped, polite or no. Many of our hosts had the pursed lips of suppressed laughter, and we felt relief when our guide pulled the bell at the bottom of the winding road into the Tcho-Tcho village. We excused ourselves as gracefully as we could, leaving small gifts and coins. I choose to believe that our guide was not proceeding away, by the time we reached the bottom of the trail, with a happy jaunt in his step. I also choose to dismiss his apparent disappointment when we called to him.

If you go, speak the language or bring a guide you trust. Avoid Leng.

—from *Travelogue*, issue 6, 1935

THE SIGN OF KNISH

The original digital defense

MAKES 30 KNISHES
PREP TIME: 15 MINUTES   **TOTAL TIME:** 40 MINUTES

THE HAND

2 large potatoes

Salt

1 medium white onion

Olive oil

Grated nutmeg

Freshly ground black pepper

All-purpose flour for dusting

One 10- by 15-inch sheet puff
   pastry

Cooking spray or unsalted butter,
   room temperature (optional)

1 egg

Mustard

THE GESTURE

○ Wash and peel the potatoes, cut them into small chunks, and boil them in salted water for about 10 minutes, until fork tender.

○ Drain the potatoes, transfer to a medium bowl, and mash them.

○ Chop the onion and sauté it, in a small pan over medium heat, in a little olive oil and a pinch of salt until the onion becomes translucent and soft.

○ Drain the oil and add the sautéed onions to the mashed potatoes. Add salt and pepper to taste and a pinch of nutmeg. Mix well and allow to cool.

○ Preheat the oven to 300°F.

○ On a flat, floured surface, unroll the pastry, stretch it, and thin it slightly with a rolling pin.

○ Spoon a 1-inch strip of the mashed mixture along the short edge. Roll the pastry over the mixture until it covers the mixture completely to form a tube with overlapping edges. Then roll it over a little more.

○ With your trusty ceremonial dagger, separate the roll from the rest of the pastry.

○ With both index fingers, press the roll into 1½-inch sections.

○ Sever the proto-knishes, one by one, and pinch the sides to form a squat cylinder. Roll it a bit in your hands to form a spheroid. The pinched sides will become top and bottom of the finished knish.

○ Spray a baking sheet with a nonstick cooking spray, grease with a little butter, or line with parchment paper.

CONTINUES

Sign of Voor Sign of Kish Sign of Koth Elder Sign Sign of Knish

- Beat the egg to create an egg wash.
- Arrange the knishes on the sheet, about an inch apart. Brush them with the prepared egg wash.
- With a syringe, piping bag, or plastic freezer bag with a corner snipped off, fill with mustard and draw the Sign of Knish on each knish.
- Bake for 10 to 12 minutes, until golden.

In Prague's Jewish Quarter, not far from the Old City, lies a medieval cemetery with more than 10,000 gravestones and several layers of burials underneath. Among the crowded rows of moss-covered tombs stands the imposing gravestone of Rabbi Judah Loew ben Bezalel, the Maharal of Prague, known for the legend of the Golem but also a famed philosopher, Talmudist, and intellectual titan of his time. Many come on pilgrimages here. Atop his headstone, people leave many folded pieces of paper—prayers, requests, and notes of gratitude—as among the stones of the Western Wall in Jerusalem. They believe Rabbi Loew, an intercessor with God, performs miracles from the afterlife. Regardless of whether you give credence to the supernatural, the magic in the air in the alleys of old Prague at dusk is undeniable, just as in Jerusalem.

You can see another gravestone in that cemetery only from a small grate at a black service door on 17th November St. It baffles visitors that they cannot see or reach the tomb from within the cemetery grounds. If you walk along the tombs looking for it, even guided by someone on the other side of the door, the grave simply is not there. Yet from that small opening on the street, it can be seen and photographed. The ancient Yiddish characters read: Berthe Katz, her birth and death dates, and an inscription that translates to "Cook of the Rabbis." Below the traditional Menorah and the Tree of Life, you'll see a highly unusual engraving: the Sign of Knish, an ancient kabbalistic gesture performed when baking.

The Al-Azif contains a rendition of the Sign of Kish, commonly associated with Saturn in gnostic magic. The Sign of Knish represents a stylized version of the older sign, easier to make with one hand while the other performs its imprint on traditional morsels. Ancient sorcerers used it for the protection of the bowels.

The wisdom books of those old traditions include several other signs, but the Sign of Knish remains unique among them in its specificity to food. Some evidence indicates that the left hand should make it while the right prepares food. Perhaps the difficulty of this arrangement symbolizes a sacrifice in the form of adversity, meant to empower the ward conveyed to those consuming the food. It is also possible that an acolyte or neophyte was meant to be present to maintain the sign. Certainly, it would not be the first time that an aspirant stood in a master's presence making a significant hand gesture.

It remains unclear how a humble cook such as Berthe Katz had access to such arcane knowledge, but apparently she gleaned it from her proximity, in a cooking capacity, to Prague's rabbinical dynasties. The mystery of her headstone also remains unsolved.

THERE CANNOLI BE ONE

Bring this tart-an delicacy to the Slavering.

SERVES THE FEW WHO REMAIN, APPROXIMATELY 6
PREP TIME: 40 MINUTES   TOTAL TIME: 1 HOUR 15 MINUTES

FROM THE DAWN OF TIME

1 box frozen puff pastry (1 sheet fully thawed)

All-purpose flour for dusting

8 tablespoons (1 stick) unsalted butter, room temperature, plus 2 tablespoons

Green and red food coloring

Coarse sugar crystals, green or color of choice

½ cup butter-flavored vegetable shortening, solid

2 cups powdered sugar

1 tablespoon vanilla extract

One 7-ounce jar marshmallow fluff

Sugar candy eyes

Slivered almonds

SCOTCH SAUCE

4 tablespoons (½ stick) unsalted butter

½ cup granulated sugar

¼ cup Scotch of choice

⅛ teaspoon ground nutmeg

1 dash salt

1 egg

THE PRIZE

◎ Preheat the oven to 400°F and line a baking sheet with parchment paper.

◎ Onto a lightly floured surface, place the thawed sheet of puff pastry and carefully unfold it.

◎ Cut the puff pastry into strips 1-inch thick. You should end up with about 8 strips.

◎ If you don't have store-bought pastry horn molds, see end of recipe for how to make your own. Starting at the narrow end of a mold, wind a pastry strip around it, down the length of the mold, overlapping the dough slightly. If needed, use a dab of water to help the dough stick to itself.

◎ Melt 2 tablespoons of butter and add a few drops of green food coloring to it.

◎ With a pastry brush, brush the green butter wash onto each horn then sprinkle it with the coarse sugar crystals.

◎ Repeat with the remaining pastry molds and strips.

◎ Place the prepared molds—large ends down, like little Christmas trees—on the parchment paper and bake for approximately 15 minutes, or until the dough just starts to turn golden. You'll be able to tell, even under the green butter.

◎ Allow them to cool to room temperature before removing the molds.

◎ While the horns are cooling, make your filling. In a stand mixer on high speed, cream the ½ cup of butter and vegetable shortening for about 5 minutes, until the mixture becomes light and fluffy.

CONTINUES

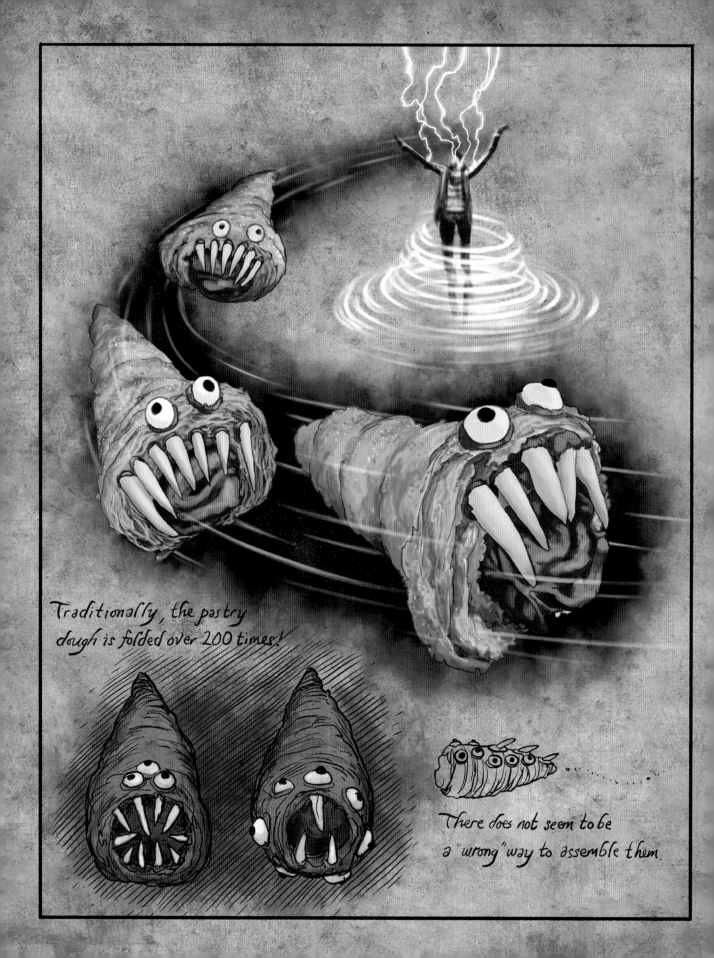

Traditionally, the pastry dough is folded over 200 times!

There does not seem to be a "wrong" way to assemble them.

- Add the powdered sugar ¼ cup at a time. Add the vanilla extract, marshmallow fluff, and enough red food coloring to turn the filling a nice, juicy red color. Scrape the sides between each addition to incorporate all ingredients thoroughly. Continue mixing for 2 more minutes.

- Transfer your red filling to a pastry bag or plastic freezer bag with a corner snipped off.

- Carefully remove the cooled horns from the molds and fill each horn with a generous amount of filling. Let it ooze out.

- Lay the horns on their sides. Use a tiny dot of red filling to affix two (or more) sugar candy eyes atop each horn.

- To give your cream spirits teeth, gently press almond slivers into the cream filling.

THE DRIZZLE

- In a small saucepan over low heat, melt the butter.

- Add remaining ingredients except the egg. Stir until all the sugar melts and the liquid is smooth.

- Remove from the heat and quickly beat in the egg, fully combining it.

- Set the saucepan over medium heat and simmer for 1 minute, at which point the sauce will thicken. Be careful that the mixture doesn't curdle.

- Drizzle the sauce over the unholy cannoli and use what remains for presentation or dipping.

Horn Molds

Cut a square of aluminum foil about 8 inches by 8 inches. Fold it in half, then in half again. Roll the reinforced foil square into a cone shape, which should be sturdy enough to hold the puff pastry and stand on its end as it bakes.

Refrigerated, the cooked horns will keep for 3 days and the Scotch Sauce for 1 week.

. . . the pastry dough folded over 200 times! The Italians didn't start making pastries like that until the Middle Ages, so where the hell did they come from? If I could verify the existence of such a confection, it would be like finding a glazed doughnut a thousand years before Dunkin' ever opened!

[. . .]

My research occasionally involved sleuthing. What I saw that night in the Silverbowl warehouse will never leave me: Two master pâtissiers hacking at each other like madmen with spatulas! Their skill was blinding, and the sky rumbled with each clash of their tools. Somewhere a radio blared a song, "Blintzes of the Universe" maybe? It didn't make sense. Nothing did that night. Back and forth they battled, their aprons shredded and spattered with blood, butter, batter.

Finally, one got the better of the other with a masterful reverse backhand slice. He beheaded his rival with a spatula! The felled pâtissier smiled as light poured from his severed neck like milk from a pitcher. The other man held his spatula before him and shuddered as if in anticipation.

Lightning struck all around. The oven glass shattered, plates and racks seemed to detonate. The victor threw his head back and shouted, "There cannoli be one!" Then a tornado of pastries engulfed him. They seemed to come alive!—all eyes and teeth, ghostly, smashing into and *through* him as he rose from the warehouse floor. I love a good Scotch, but I wasn't drinking that night. Those cannoli are the only evidence I have. I left the head and took the cannoli.

—extract from *A Mental Urge: My History of Ancient Pastry-Making* by Brenda W., p. 225

TRI-LOBE BITES

Poppable mozzarella balls with a mélange of flavors. Here's looking at you, squid.

SERVES 6 OR 9
PREP TIME: 15 MINUTES   **TOTAL TIME:** 25 MINUTES

THE MASKS

3 ounces yellow mustard

1 ounce white Zinfandel

1 ounce Worcestershire sauce

1 lime

25 ciliegine ("cherry size")
   mozzarella balls, room
   temperature

1 pomegranate or package of
   pomegranate arils

Balsamic glaze

THE THREE-LOBED BURNING EYE!

- In a small bowl, mix the mustard, wine, and Worcestershire sauce. Set aside.

- Zest the lime.

- With a knife, cut an opening in each mozzarella ball, then finger the opening to create a deep cavity. Sprinkle the outsides of the balls with lime zest.

- Spoon a small portion of the mustard-wine sauce into each of the cavities. Reserve the remaining sauce for presentation or dipping.

- Carefully insert three pomegranate seeds into each cavity.

- Place one drop of balsamic glaze over the seeds to glaze the eyes.

- Refrigerate for 1 hour and serve cold.

Why I hadn't thought to preside over the provisioning of comestibles at events of moment, I cannot say. But it came to Me, as one mortal who imagined himself steeped in the knowledge of Those Who Went Before bumbled through a rite of joining back in elder Mu, that I could help.

What makes a memorable gathering, wedding, graduation, or mass sacrifice? Why, it's the food of course!—six or seven courses, as in modern custom. We offer scores of recipes, from drinks to desserts. There's even a kids menu.

Imagine My delight at discovering that dozens, even hundreds at once, would ingest whatever madness and debauchery I created, eagerly and with gusto, if only some dead-eyed servant in formal clothing served it on a silver platter! Wonderful!

At affairs of high state, My eyes could be placed in the bellies of the most powerful and influential. They could be Mine with just a bit of mustard and fermented liquescence! In turn, My zest for corruption could be theirs with no more effort than the gathering of needful things and some simple preparation. Why strain to speak with other's tongues when whole mouths could be Mine so completely and easily?

Yes, We here at Nyarlath-on-Tap foresee with three-lobed sight Our presence at any gathering of merit or the meritorious. Why use some ignominious upstart food service when you could have a Great Old One? Make your next gathering the incoherent talk of the town. It will be a night your guests cannot forget!

Weddings • Bar/Bat Mitzvahs • Graduations • State Functions • Sweet Sixteens • Apotheosis

—vision statement of Nyarlath-on-Tap Premium Catering Services

TSATHOGGUA-CAMOLE

Toadally awesome bacon guacamole

SERVES 10 TO 12 HUMANOIDS
PREP TIME: 30 MINUTES　　**TOTAL TIME:** 45 MINUTES

INTO THE CAULDRON

2 medium plum tomatoes

¼ red onion

5 baby corns

5 slices bacon

4 avocados, ripe

1 tablespoon lime juice

¼ cup cilantro (optional)

1 teaspoon paprika

Sea salt and freshly ground black
　pepper

SSSSERVE

0 Preheat the oven to 400°F.

0 While the oven is heating, dice the tomatoes and onion and quarter the baby corns lengthwise.

0 Cook the bacon for 15 to 18 minutes. Allow it to cool, then crumble it.

0 If using uncooked baby corns, boil them in 1 inch of water until limp, remove, and allow to cool.

0 While the bacon is cooking and corn quarters are boiling, extract the avocado flesh and transfer it to a medium glass bowl.

0 Add the lime juice and mash the avocado flesh until smooth.

0 Into the guacamole, mix all the ingredients except the baby corn quarters. Season with salt and pepper to taste.

0 If using precooked baby corn, microwave the quarters for 15 seconds.

0 Garnish the guacamole with the corn quarter tentacles and serve with tortilla chips.

0 N'Kai-ndly tell everyone where you found this recipe.

Great inverted snub icosidodecahedron – Cthulhu $s5/3s3s$

Snub icosidodecadodecahedron – Dagon $s5/3s3s5*a$

Great snub dodecicosidodecahedron – Shub-Niggurath $s5/3s5/2s3*a$

Great retrosnub icosidodecahedron – Azathoth $s5/3s3/2s$

Small retrosnub icosicosidodecahedron – Yog-Sothoth $s5/2s3/2s3/2*a$

Snub dodecahedron – Chaugner Faugn – $s5/2s5s$

Great snub icosidodecahedron – Tsathoggua $s5/2s3s$

Small snub icosicosidodecahedron – Hastur $s5/2,3s3*a$

Inverted snub dodecadodecahedron – Nyarlathotep $s5/3s5s$

I foller'd them what bin stealin' me peppers an' me green beauties. Dark it were, or I'da seen through their disguise sooner an' I'da not come here. Now's too late. Trapped I am in this red-lit Hell under me own land. These corridors wind f'rever, an' I'm turnt aroun' but good. Them robes, knew they's too long! Bas'ards don' sway like they's dancin' ta some rhydd'm. They ain't gots no feet! Snakes them are from the wais' down. The sway's jes them movin'. Shoulda knowed by the tracks, smoothed an' all. Thought they's covrin' 'em with booms or sommat, too big ta see 'em for wha' they were. No snake's that big, none I ev'r seen or heared of.

Down, down, two days I slunk behin' 'em. Drinkin' wall water an' a-chewin' on what I brought ta keep up me strength. Two days, down an' down. When the floor stopped bein' all konkywonkus, we was in a big cave, real big. Blocks of stone, huge an' all around, like it mebbe use' ta be more reg'lar. Like a city of snakes, deep in the ground. I dunno where we are, could be under the mountain by now. I reck'n we trended that way.

They's bringin' all what they a-stole from me ta what looked like this great cauldron. I know I seen somethin' like that in a old book I wasn' s'posed ta be lookin' in. But this was . . . alive. Man oh man, did I let out a yelp of fright! A'first, I thought I's a dead'un right then, but then I 'memberd snakes gots no ears! Lucky for me . . . or mebbe they's knew I's there all along but din't care none.

They put the last in, an' th' thing was done chewin' it all together. Then they dipped spoons an' bowls in the mess. Some was even brave ta go right up an' dip whatever they's eatin' the stuff on right inna that mouth! E'r once a while, these 'orrible sucker-ropes, like a octopus got, shot out an' grabbed one o' 'em. They all paused a moment, the one in the gold hood hissed some'in' a while, an' they wint back t' it like nuthin' happened. I never wanna see any of that agin, but I writ it all down—case they ever find me an' you see a red glow deep in a cave near these parts. You go on back, ya hear? Maybe leave 'em some peppers an' avocados an' such so they don't come lookin' for 'em.

—handwritten note found on the desiccated body of an avocado farmer in [redacted], 1924

UBBO-SALSA

Primordial dipping sludges for the patient and those hastening to immerse themselves

INGREDIENTS

1 small bunch green onions
1 medium green bell pepper
1 medium yellow bell pepper
Sunflower or corn oil
1 garlic clove
Salt and freshly ground black
  pepper
2 or 3 teaspoons apple cider
  vinegar
Lime juice (optional)

DEVOLUTION

◐ Wash the green onions and pat dry. Cut off the roots with 1 inch of the stalks and set aside. Use the rest of the white stalks for another dish, such as the Hen-Thai Corn Tacos (page 93). Trim the green leaves 6 inches from the ends, reserving the rest of the green leaves for the next step, and set aside.

◐ Halve, core, and deseed the peppers. Remove the inner membranes. Finely chop the peppers and the reserved green onion leaves from the prior step.

◐ In a small frying pan over medium heat, sauté all the chopped green onion leaves and three-quarters of the peppers in a little oil until they soften.

◐ Season with salt and pepper to taste, remove the pan from the heat, and allow it cool to room temperature.

◐ Add the remaining one-quarter of the raw chopped peppers, 1 tablespoon of oil, apple cider vinegar to taste, and a splash of lime juice, if using. Mix well and set the salsa aside.

◐ Over the rim of a white serving bowl, drape the reserved 6-inch green onion leaves. Spoon the cooked salsa into the white serving bowl so the green onion leaves emerge from the sludge, like excrescences sprouting from the primordial Ubbo-Salsa.

CONTINUES

"There, in the green of the produce market and the depths of the shelves, the incomplete mass of Ubbo-Salsa lurked—waiting the Time of Combination.

Headless onions, peppers without seem or seed, juices and oils comingling and astir... the colors of life unrecognized, waiting to nourish her own descendants..."
—"Ubbo-Salsa", Clerk Aisle Sixth

Tomatillo the Intermediate

Verde the Mild

Chimichurri the Cilantrous

These can't be their real names!

- Garnish with the reserved green onion roots.
- Serve with Atlach-Nachos from *The Necronomnomnom* (page 34) or chips of choice.

> This salsa works wonders as a relish for barbecue staples such as hamburgers, chitlins, etc.!

UBBO-EASY EVOLUTION

3 green onions, chopped

12 chives, cut in half

One 16-ounce jar salsa verde, mild

One 16-ounce jar tomatillo salsa, medium

One 12½-ounce jar chimichurri salsa

¼ teaspoon ground mustard

¼ teaspoon turmeric

- Chop the green onions and halve the chives.
- In a large bowl, combine all ingredients except the chives and mix well.
- Transfer to a serving bowl and garnish with the chive halves inserted vertically and chaotically.
- Refrigerate the remains.

Investigators remain baffled about the disappearance of Ben Kincaid, 39, of Ashton, last seen at the Veg-O-Mart on Smith Street on July 12.

On July 11, Kincaid entered the market, walked to the produce section, and examined an arrangement of green and yellow bell peppers. On several occasions, a store clerk (who requested anonymity for this article) asked Kincaid whether he needed any assistance. After several hours, Kincaid departed the store without incident.

On the day of his disappearance, security footage shows Kincaid entering the market at 9:36 p.m., again walking to the produce section, where for several minutes he examined a display of greens. After a glitch, the video garbles for a few seconds. When it resumes, Kincaid is no longer in frame, but police confirm that no other security cameras in the store or on the street record him leaving.

Investigators found a piece of parchment at Kincaid's apartment and have released it, in its entirety, to *The Ashton-Picayune*.

> *There, in the green of the produce market and the depths of the shelves, the incomplete mass of Ubbo-Salsa lurked, waiting for the Time of Combination. Headless onions, peppers sans seams or seeds, juices and oils comingling and astir. The colors of life unrecognized, waiting to nourish her own descendants.*
>
> *—"Ubbo-Salsa," Clerk Aisle Sixth*

Police have contacted the Ashton Public Library for clarification but, at time of press, had not heard back. If you have any leads about this text or Kincaid's whereabouts, please contact the Ashton Police Department.

—newsclip from *The Ashton-Picayune*, August 7, 1977

SALT AND

BATTER-Y

SALMON 'WICH TILES

Suffer not the fish to swim with these unjustly delicious snack squares.

SERVES 9
PREP TIME: 10 MINUTES   **TOTAL TIME:** 20 MINUTES

WILD ACCUSATIONS

9 slices bacon

1 large cucumber

4 ounces smoked salmon

3 ounces cream cheese

THE VERDICT

⓪ Preheat the oven to 400°F.

⓪ Cook the bacon for 15 to 18 minutes and allow it to cool.

⓪ While the bacon is cooking, peel the cucumber and slice the salmon into strips.

⓪ Cover the salmon strips with cream cheese and roll in wax paper. Keep the paper out of the roll.

⓪ Freeze the salmon cream cheese roll for 30 minutes.

⓪ While the roll is freezing, trim the peeled cucumber into a cuboid (square cross-section), then cut it into square slices.

⓪ Slice the roll into ½-inch wheels.

⓪ Stack the salmon cream cheese wheels between cucumber squares, wrap bacon around both, and secure with a toothpick.

⓪ Refrigerate until ready to serve.

- rolling the creamcheese and salmon w/waxed paper.

What heathenry is this?
Fish and Swine?

Skinned,
baked,
spread,
impaled —
such are the wages
of sin!

APPARITOR: *Be it recorded that thou, goode and renowned Hawk of witchery, hast witnessed the accused of Combinations most untoward and strange in her preparations for our Gracious and Noble Avowry. Is this so, Sir Alestaire?*

CRUMM: *Aye! 'Tis the naked Truth! Conjoin did she swine, fish, the product of udders a'firm'd and pliant, and the harvest of the field!*

APPARITOR: *Calm thyself, Witchfinder. The accused standeth secure. The Courte calleth I the Back'us Boy to provide testimony. Boy, didst thou see this alleged unholy combination of all manner of Bounty from sea and field?*

BACK'US BOY: *I-I did, m'lord. Verily she made me to cook the Bacone to perfection and yet spared me none of it, though my stomach did grumble like a Beast in the hedge!*

CRUMM: *Perfection! Who hath such methods, to pass such Skill to a mere child with a single lesson? Witchery!*

APPARITOR: *Hold thee thy tongue, Witchfinder, lest the Bailiff do it for thee! Goode use of the Herd is no crime, nor denying the boy a bounty not his by right. Hoggard MacSorely, tell the Courte thine account.*

MACSORELY: *She bought all me best pigs, she did. Had the Devil's eye for it. Always the best, every time.*

CRUMM: *He hath seen it! He hath seen it in her eye! The Devil! More than the salmon should be Smoked! Like her damnable delectables, she should be skinned, baked, spread, and impaled! Such are the wages of sin!*

APPARITOR: *As the Lord is our witness, thou hast cinched the buckle of thine hat too tightly, Nathaniel! Bailiff, remove him! We must assay the seized comestible which goode Seamus Belhoste hath kept for the purpose.*

BELHOST: *By my trothe, half have vanished into the thin air!*

APPARITOR: *What salmon-colored crumb lieth in thy beard, Belhost?*

BELHOST: *Why, m'lord, I did seek only to . . . uh . . . appraise the safety of these Morsels before the Courte. Some unknown Power did move me to it!*

APPARITOR: *Aye, it hovers now betwixt thine ample breast and straining belt. Thou mayst go. The Courte standeth adjourned.*

[Adjournment for evidentiary examination]

APPARITOR: *The Courte findeth these offerings unconventional but wholesome. The Accused standeth free of Guilt, though her creation may not. Moderation in all things, goode People; including Moderation.*

—court records, testimony of Nathaniel J. Crumm, witchfinder, Salem, Province of Massachusetts Bay, 1693

A-TACOLYPSE

Desperate times call for desperate pleasures.

SERVES 6 TO 12 DENIZENS OF THE CYCLOPEAN WASTES
PREP TIME: 20 MINUTES   **TOTAL TIME:** 30 MINUTES

SCAVENGED FROM THE RUINS

12 hot dogs

1 large tomato

3 to 4 ounces jalapeño peppers, fresh or pickled

12 hard taco shells

Ketchup

Yellow mustard

4 to 6 ounces shredded Mexican cheese blend

Shredded lettuce

6 to 8 ounces salsa of choice

NEW CUSTOMS

◎ Cook the hot dogs in manner of preference.

◎ While the hot dogs are cooking, dice the tomato and slice the peppers.

◎ Place one hot dog in each taco shell.

◎ Adorn with ketchup and mustard to taste.

◎ Atop the condimented hot dogs, layer cheese, lettuce, and tomato. Tuck the pepper slices along the top and top with salsa.

◎ Serve while the hot dogs are hot.

Last night, the Book showed me a vision of a burning city, my hometown, crawling with monstrosities of all sizes. Crawling, stomping, slithering, flapping, burrowing and oozing through the falling, burning, vanishing world of man. Oh, the crying, the screaming, the agony, the hanging odor of burning flesh, the lack of silverware, the inappropriate condiments!

In the end, the desperate, fleeing masses will feed upon anything they can find, consuming unthinkable combinations. I say, why wait until the end?

The plague brought the world to a screeching halt. No one knew if our reaction was too much or not enough. We had only the media's lurid coverage and alarmed communications from friends in the Hot Zones.

We had rations in the larders, so we were less affected and cooler-headed. As a world used to near-infinite variety and instant gratification shuddered under forced shutdowns and isolation orders, our hidden hilltop kept chaos at bay. We watched, waited, and ate sparingly of our best stores.

In time, horrors of nature and mankind accelerated in frequency and amplified in magnitude. Distant travel for provisions became inadvisable. We became creative with meals, mixing elements that nature and culture never intended. They sustained us.

A recurring staple reflected what was happening in the cities of Man. The outer shell hardened but remained brittle. Within, the rich mix of ingredients mostly harmonized—unexpectedly. The core was soft and processed. The red splashed and spattered at times, but some things were necessary.

We eat them now, these clashing creations born of hardship, because our palates have mutated to crave them in the wake of the virus and to remind ourselves of what still lurks out there. The need may come again, and we will be ready.

—based on a true story

As this recipe came to me from Salem (at great cost) complete with that not-so-subtle name, my guess is has something to do with the Deep Ones' rumored control of the Shoggoths.

If my theory is correct, it may very well be in our best interest to make A LOT of this stuff!

BROCCOLI-LI

Baked broccoli tempura with dipping sauce will call to you.

SERVES 5
PREP TIME: 25 MINUTES   **TOTAL TIME:** 38 MINUTES

THE PRIMORDIALS

Unsalted butter for greasing
1 chalice seasoned crumbs of
   bread
Salt
3 unborn fowl
1 lime
½ cup Kedem 100 percent grape
   juice
5 cups broccoli florets, rinsed
   and slightly moist
¼ cup flour for all purposes

THE FLORETS FOR THE TREES

0 Preheat the oven to 450°F and grease a large baking sheet with butter.

0 In a shallow bowl, commingle the breadcrumbs with salt to taste.

0 In a separate bowl, whisk the eggs together.

0 Into a third bowl, juice the lime and add the grape juice. Set aside.

0 In a large bowl or sealed plastic freezer bag, toss the tiny trees to and fro with all your might, coating them in the flour of the fields. Shake from them any excess.

0 Into the egg bath, dip the tiny trees but do not coat their trunks.

0 Twirl each tree in the seasoned crumbs to coat lightly. Shake off any excess.

0 Thus prepared, place them onto the buttered baking sheet but stack them not!

0 Oven them for 12 to 13 minutes, turning occasionally. When done, the enrobed crowns shall have turned golden brown.

0 Plate them and drizzle them violetly with juices.

0 Save any remnant liquid for dipping.

0 As your hunger crescendos, cry aloud: *Broccoli-li! Broccoli-li!*

Deep in a sacred trance, within my crystal of obsidian did I behold the Forest Primeval. My Enochian guides had brought me to a place of sublime tranquility, untouched by Man, for he existed not at this time. For hours did I observe the comings and goings of strange birds and beasts of the ground. The mighty trees swayed gently, and the sky shone a cerulean so deep that only a Herculean exertion of will took my eyes from it. Why had my guides chosen this time and place for my customary revelation? Certes, the tone and flavor changed then. In the distance, lightnings grew and reached down to touch what at first I took to be a strange low cloud, so large was it, and so completely did it blot the horizon of my past. Mottled brown and gold, this presence crashed like a wave upon the forest. Its substance enwrapped the emerald tops of the trees, and it used them to pull itself forward into my view. Horrid limbs of no natural flesh formed and dissolved as it engulfed the upper reaches of the woodland. A flight of strange and beautiful birds, four of wing and eye, turned as one to flee the fell abomination, but even the freedom of the unspoiled sky gave no proof against its power. Limbs lashed skyward for them as I watched, and in horror did I see these beauteous feathered forefathers of our avian species crushed like so many grapes. Rain the color of porphyry fell upon the mass of it below, where the skin of what wrapped around the top of every tree drank it in. In shocked dismay, I watched, frozen, until it reached the cusp of my vista, and reaching for me through the crystal came a primordial cry from the thousand mouths it formed to scream: Broccoli-li! Broccoli-li!

—modernized writings of E. Kelley, 1587

CARNI-S'MORES

A primal pleaser worthy of Caesar

SERVES 2 TO 3
PREP TIME: 10 MINUTES   **TOTAL TIME:** 30 MINUTES

WHAT'S AT STEAK

One 12- to 16-ounce New York
   strip steak
¼ teaspoon smoked paprika
¼ teaspoon onion powder
¼ teaspoon garlic powder
¼ teaspoon freshly ground black
   pepper
2 tablespoons unsalted butter
12 slices thick-cut bacon

GRILL IT WITH FIRE!

1. Cut the steak into 12 cubes.

2. In a small bowl, combine the spices and mix thoroughly.

3. Melt the butter and add to the spice mixture.

4. Wrap a slice of bacon completely around each steak cube in both directions. Secure the wrapped cubes with skewers.

5. Brush the skewered cubes with the spiced butter.

6. Roast over wood of choice (hickory or sassafras suggested) until done to preference.

Surely, a primitive recipe.
Meat and meat and fire.

meat
within
meat.

Burnhenge, where the
remains and personal belongings
of O. Baer and A——, my
mentor in dark culinary
were found in 1995.

over 20 years
after they
disappeared——

POLICE REPORT

DATE [SMUDGED, ILLEGIBLE]

CASE #WT31-3: 03-38-331-38

RESPONDING OFFICER(S): Corp. Anderson

INCIDENT: At approximately 10:31 p.m., Wilbert Busdruple called to report a fire at a nearby residence. He explained that no structures were involved. FD not dispatched. On arrival, Corp. Anderson observed two males enjoying a controlled campfire, accompanied by what Anderson called "the most alluring aroma I ever smelled." The males, unidentified members of the Retals family, were roasting skewered meats over the fire. Anderson characterized them as "cheerfully irritated," complaining that "Some folk just can't let others live. That's most of what's wrong with people today." Anderson notes that the Retals property is not viewable directly from the Busdruple estate and questions whether the observation itself constitutes a violation. Trying to deduce whether the comestibles came from unlicensed hunting on the Busdruple property, Anderson asked the provenance of the meat. One of the Retals men handed him a skewer and said, "Test it as you like. Try it with some of this barbeque sauce." Andersen reports that "the meat was good-quality beef wrapped in seasoned bacon" but doesn't explain how he made this determination with such certainty. At the station, dark stains observed on his uniform lapel may not allow for objective conclusions.

ACTION TAKEN: No violation noted, no citation issued.

FOLLOW-UP: Anderson vigorously maintains that this activity may constitute some weekend ritual of the Retals household. He has requested permission to surveil the Retals property on Friday and Saturday nights to confirm his suspicion. The chief granted permission to him and other officers on duty, in rotation, ordering that sufficient samples from local delis be obtained for testing the Retals method.

—nuisance complaint from a police report prepared by Sgt. Fenton
in [redacted], Pennsylvania

HOUNDS AND TENDERLOUPES

Cocktail weenies and cantaloupe wrapped in bacon? It's a trap!

YIELDS 15 TO 20 DISTRACTINGLY YUMMY MOUTHFULS
PREP TIME: 40 MINUTES   **TOTAL TIME:** 1 HOUR 20 MINUTES

THE PARTS OF THE SNARE

1 pound bacon

1 cantaloupe

Brown sugar

One 14-ounce package cocktail weenies or mini hot dogs

Dark Karo syrup

Sea salt

TO MAKE YOUR ESCAPE

0. Preheat the oven to 400°F.

0. Cook the bacon for 5 minutes (not crispy) and let it cool to room temperature.

0. While the bacon is cooking and cooling, cut the cantaloupe into approximately 40 cuboids roughly ¼ by ¼ by 3 inches. They should resemble French fries.

0. Line a baking sheet with parchment paper. Spoon ½ teaspoon of brown sugar onto the paper. Repeat 15 to 20 times, evenly spacing the piles and not spooning any against the edges.

0. Place two rods of cantaloupe on either side of a cocktail weenie, then wrap one slice of bacon around the trio. The cocktail weenie should stick out from the bacon on one side. Impale the hounds upon a toothpick to secure the morsels.

0. Onto the lined baking sheet, place each uncooked hound atop a pile of brown sugar, drizzle with Karo syrup, and sprinkle with sea salt.

0. Cook for 12 to 14 minutes on a higher rack.

0. Increase the heat and broil for 3 more minutes, until the tops just start to char. Be careful that the parchment paper doesn't catch fire.

0. Allow to cool for 10 minutes.

0. Pick up the hound bites to drain any excess liquid, then transfer to a serving plate.

I have never seen the Hounds of Tindalos, nor have I ever heard a reliable, much less accurate, description of one. I just began drawing and the Book did the rest, I think. But the Book has misled me before!

I've heard that the hound's proboscis is a long, hollow tongue, but I think that it is more similar to that of the assassin bug.

but who has seen one and survived?

Don't bother with trying to round off all the corners in your home. — there's ALWAYS an angle.

That fool Juan, over in Providence, has no idea what he's doing. Now that these damned hounds are hunting us both, thanks to <u>him</u>, I may not even share my discovery. Let him "go to the dogs," I say!

The melonic convergence is critical. They don't enter our world already of a particular size. They adjust their stature and mass when they arrive. Physically it's quite fascinating. This ability from whatever strange world from which they originate can work to our advantage.

The spherical melons are perfect! Only a small, baited aperture is necessary, and the beasts can be trapped. Both bacon and brown sugar seem to work and, combined, they prove irresistible. The whole then can be collapsed on the invader and fixed with simple wooden stakes. More of the strips infused with essential saltes complete the trap. They're sort of adorable when so small and helpless. But who would've thought that they could travel in such large packs? No matter. The limbs shrivel with the heat but given time they regenerate. One more step renders safety for any length of . . . Time. I hesitate to record it for fear of being thought mad, but the whole procedure becomes useless without the last part of the protocol.

To banish the pack until more arrive whence they come—a process that apparently takes weeks or months—they need to be . . . <u>eaten</u>. Yes, yes, I know! One might think them inimical to life from our world, but they're delicious! Prepared this way, they remain perfectly safe as an occasional indulgence born of necessity. I've felt no ill effects and have no indication that they lack nourishing elements easily handled by the human constitution. They go quite well with the components of their containment, and cooking renders them quite unable to retaliate. It's important, though, to capture them as they enter our dimension. The spheroids must be ready so they don't become too large too quickly once properly oriented.

Clearly my design is far superior to Juan's. It doesn't merely trap them, it dissolves them! Ha! Let them come! I'll be peckish for their flesh again by then.

—lab notes discovered in the wreckage of a chemist's workshop
on an Arkham estate, 1936

HUMMUS SACRISPICE

A spicy statement on the hummus condition: gonzo garbanzos rediscovered by Alonzo

SERVES 5 TO 10
TOTAL TIME: 20 MINUTES

GRIST FOR THE MILL

½ cup lemon juice
4 tablespoons ricotta
4 cups canned chickpeas
1 small bunch chives
1 small bunch green onions
1 small chipotle pepper or 1
   tablespoon cayenne pepper
4 garlic cloves
1 teaspoon coriander
1 teaspoon cumin
Sea salt and freshly ground black
   pepper
2 to 4 ounces shelled edamame
   (soybeans)

BEAN THERE, DONE THAT

❶ In a food processor, add the lemon juice, ricotta, and chickpeas and puree.

❷ Add all remaining ingredients except the edamame and puree again thoroughly.

❸ Transfer to a serving bowl, garnish with the edamame, and serve with pita or crunchy chips of choice.

Do not attempt to offer your Sacrispice w/out also including appropriate chippage or scraps of bread.

Culture Column

The ruined structures of Calixtlahuaca stand as a testament to the brilliance of the Aztec peoples. But less well known today is that, before the Aztecs, who conquered the region in the 1400s, the Matlatzinca people originally lived here.

Records indicate that Aztec nobles were horrified and inspired by the worship practiced there. Their sages advised them that the wisest course of action was to continue the most prominent rites in order to placate the local gods and powerful spirits.

The Tablets of Garban'Zoh describe how the legs of many servants of the priesthood powered the great stones within the main structure, turning cleverly designed slabs of rock at varying angles. Into the pit where this apparatus lay high priests threw sacrificial victims drawn from the ranks of political enemies, criminals, and others selected by the Matlatzincza and Aztec peoples to serve society better this way than in life.

Scientists have detected traces of pepper, coriander, and cumin on the broken slabs, a stark reminder of the importance placed on such rituals. The indigenous peoples of the time considered these and other spices more precious than gold. Linguists recently clarified one of the most horrifying parts of this practice, child sacrifice, as a mistranslation. The Spanish verb *soy* is of course an exact cognate for the beans garnishing the spiced paste, the main product of the sacrifice. This writer can only imagine the consternation of the Esperanto enthusiasts who, at the time of the discovery of the writings and carvings of Calixtlahuaca, read that particular ingredient as "I am beans." It brings to mind the old joke: "What's a monster's favorite type of beans? Human beans!"

Oh, the delicious human capacity for humor in the face of absolute horror.

—A. Typer, *El Sol de Toluca*, April 1964

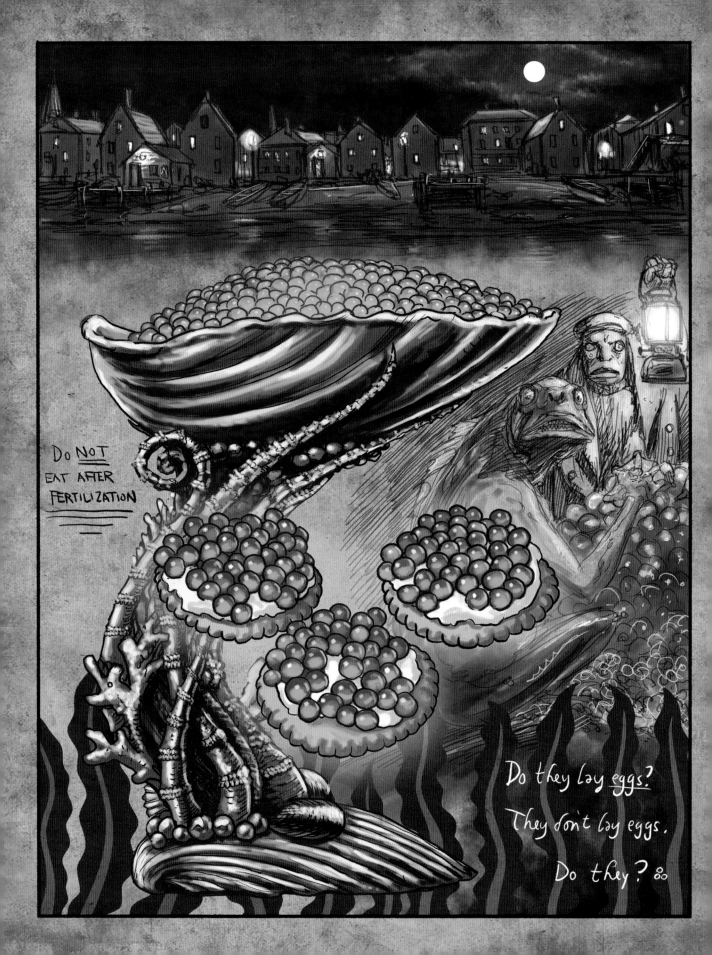

JNNSMOUTH ROE

Who doesn't love a roe-mantic walk down the beach?

SERVES MOTHER HYDRA AND ALL HER FAVORED
PREP TIME: 15 MINUTES   **TOTAL TIME:** 60 MINUTES

DEEP CHEMISTRY

2 teaspoons calcium chloride
(CaCl$_2$) or calcium lactate
(C$_6$H$_{10}$CaO$_6$)

1 or 2 cubes bouillon of choice
(chicken, veggie, or shrimp)

20 to 30 drops green food
coloring,

1 or 2 teaspoons sodium alginate
(C$_6$H$_9$NaO$_7$)

CALIBRATE THE SPAWNING

1. In a large bowl, add 3 cups of cold water and the calcium reactive. Blend thoroughly with a hand mixer for 1 minute.

2. In a small saucepan, boil 2 cups of water with bouillon. The broth should taste robust and intense. Through a sieve, filter the broth. Refrigerate for 30 minutes.

3. Transfer the mixture to a wide bowl, add food coloring, and blend. Add the alginate, blend well, and let it rest for about 10 minutes.

4. Draw 1 teaspoon of the green concoction with a food syringe (no needle) and position it over the calcium water bath. Press the plunger *slowly*, releasing one drop at a time into the water. Avoid spurting long strands. Using two syringes will allow you to double your efforts.

5. With the sieve, capture a few test roe to see whether they retain their spherical shape. If they collapse, add 1 more teaspoon of alginate to the green broth and blend again. Let it rest and repeat the test. A higher concentration of alginate will help the roe retain its shape.

6. Frequently collect the stable roe with the sieve, lightly rinse, and transfer to a serving bowl. Repeat until you finish the broth.

7. Refrigerate the roe until ready to serve.

8. Serve atop light cream cheese spread over saltine crackers or, for an unreal touch of realism, present on a bed of seaweed.

EXT: BEACH, FULL MOON—NIGHT

GREG

All right, we're at Innsmouth Nursery Cove, as locals call it. It's on the beach, south of town.

CUT TO:

WE SEE the moonlit sea, and an ominous reef not far from the coast, town lights in the distance.

CUT TO:

GREG (CONT'D)

We were told this is the right place and tonight's the right time to film the secret ritual of the Deep Ones laying their eggs in the seaweed beds, which lie only 30 or 40 feet from shore in just knee-deep water. We saw it clearly this morning. Under the sun, the stench was awful. Now it's not so bad. OK, Tim, let's lie low and wait.

THE CAMERA JERKS as Tim affixes it to a tripod and points it toward the beach. Across the dark ocean, waves carry moonlit foam ashore. After a few minutes, we hear the indecipherable sounds of Tim and Greg arguing. Several figures move along the shore.

GREG (V.O.)

Here they come! Look, Tim! Here they come! OK, OK, let's be quiet. Let's try zooming in a bit.

THE CAMERA ZOOMS to a close-up of one of the creatures, wading into the sea.

TIM (V.O.)

Wow, that's awesome. They're squatting. Looks like they're going to lay their—

GREG (V.O., interrupting)

—Oh man, the stench is back. Ugh, that's disgusting. But the wind is blowing out to sea. Wait, is it coming from behind us?

A MOMENT OF SILENCE before the camera jerks to the side, pointing to the sky. We hear bloodcurdling screams suddenly cut short. The remaining video, about 25 minutes, shows the night sky, stars going in and out of focus, as the wind occasionally blows sounds of joyful squealing ashore.

—transcription of found footage from the cold case files of the Massachusetts State Police.

The MicroSD card, commonly used in photo cameras circa 2010, features an .AVI video file.

The card label reads "INNS.BEACH 2018/03/06" in minuscule type.

Joe Sargent's Poppers Lonely Heartichoke Club Sandwich

We hope you will enjoy the chow.

SERVES 2 DEEPLY

PREP TIME: 20 MINUTES   **TOTAL TIME:** 20 MINUTES

HIGH NOTES

8 jalapeño poppers

1 tablespoon mayonnaise

1 tablespoon ranch dressing

½ teaspoon chipotle seasoning

4 slider-sized rolls

Shredded lettuce of choice

4 artichoke hearts

2 plum tomatoes

THE ENSEMBLE

Ⓞ Strike up the brand and cook the poppers according to package directions.

Ⓞ In a small bowl, combine the mayonnaise, dressing, and seasoning. Stir well.

Ⓞ Separate the tops and bottoms of the rolls and spread with the chipotle ranch dressing.

Ⓞ To the two bottom halves, add shredded lettuce and then two poppers, flatter sides up.

Ⓞ Top or destem the artichoke hearts if necessary. Parallel with the stem and starting in the middle, cut the hearts open.

Ⓞ Cut two slices from each tomato. Place each cut heart over a tomato slice and splay the petals open onto the tomato. Cap the hearts with the top halves of the slider rolls, holding them together with a toothpick.

Ⓞ Place the roll-capped artichoke heart and tomato slice onto the poppers and push the toothpick all the way down for serving.

Ⓞ Remove the toothpicks and compress the slider for ease of consumption.

Sargent Is a Loathly Carp-Head Man

It was many moons ago today
Joseph Sargent struck the land in bay.
He's been going to and from the isle,
Which is only off the shore a mile,
So, mayo introduced to you,
a fact you've known for all these years:
Sargent is a loathly carp-head man!

Joe Sargent is a loathly carp-head man.
You've seen the coastal waters glow.
Sargent is a loathly carp-head man.
Lean back and let the ammo blow.
Sargent is a loathly, Sargent is a loathly,
Sargent is a loathly carp-head man!

He's guttural and quite queer.
He has such horrid gills.
Calls Dagon through clairaudience.
He'd like to take us home with him.
He'd love to take us home.

Oh you really may not wanna know
They wanna fill you with their roe.
Now the siren's gonna sing a song,
So pray hard that all the stars are wrong
Or Joe will introduce to you
To one of humankind's worst fears.
Sargent is a loathly carp-head man!

THE SNACKS OF ULTHAR

Hush Kitties

FEEDS 2 HUMANS OR 4 ULTHARIANS
PREP TIME: 1 HOUR 15 MINUTES   TOTAL TIME: 1 HOUR 30 MINUTES

THE CAT-ALOG

1 medium to large potato

Salt

Sunflower oil

1 small white onion

One 12-ounce can tuna in oil or
water, drained and shredded
(for 8 ounces of tuna)

1 egg, plus 1 egg yolk

1 teaspoon garlic powder

½ teaspoon sweet paprika

½ teaspoon ginger powder

1 pinch granulated sugar

1 pinch freshly ground black
pepper

¾ to 1 cup cornflakes

THE TALL TAIL

0. Peel the potato, cut it into small chunks, and boil it in lightly salted water for 10 minutes or until tender.

0. While the potato is cooking, finely dice the onion and, in a small frying pan over medium heat, add a little sunflower oil and sauté the onion until golden.

0. Drain and mash the potato and drain the oil from the onion.

0. To the mashed potato, add the sautéed onion, the tuna, the egg and yolk, the spices, and ½ teaspoon salt. Mix well until all blends together. Set aside.

0. Into a paper or plastic bag, add the cornflakes and crush them with a rolling pin to make a coarse breading powder.

0. Spoon 1 tablespoon balls of tuna-potato mix, roll them in the cornflake crumbs to coat, arrange them on a tray, and refrigerate for 1 hour.

0. In sunflower oil, fry the balls in small batches, 3 to 4 minutes per side, until golden.

0. Remove the balls from the oil and let them rest on a wire rack lined with paper towels.

0. Serve warm or cold and don't play with your food. No one wants to find one of these under the couch.

~ It is said that in Ulthar, which lies beyond the river Skai, these fried tuna bites are a coveted delicacy, and this I can verily believe, as I proceed to devour a whole saucer of them while sitting by the fire. Alas, my many cats are not allowed to partake in them, and I am forced to turn deaf ears to their pleas. For although this recipe calls for their favorite staple fish, its preparation requires exotic seasonings... saltes and spices which are noxious to their delicate feline constitutions. I wonder if they understand my explanations when I deny them a piece of this delicious snack. For the cat is cryptic, and lately, I seem to notice a conspiratorial air in their conversations, as if they were plotting to overpower me in my sleep and make ME their dinner...

Well, a cat worshiper like myself should proudly aspire to be so consumed. A true apotheosis, the ultimate communion between feline and man.

Perhaps tonight —

After receiving calls from neighbors reporting that they hadn't seen the old man walking down the street, followed by some of his cats, as it was his daily custom, police broke into the decrepit house. Inside they found his skeleton, picked clean, lying on his bed, perfectly dressed in old-fashioned pajamas. No signs of struggle were evident, as if, whatever gruesome fate befell him, he received it with quiet resignation—or perhaps with joy, judging by the terrifying, triumphant smile of his skull. Herewith is the last entry from his diary, which might shed light on what happened that frightful night.

It is said that in Ulthar, which lies beyond the river Skai, these fried tuna bites are a coveted delicacy, and this I can believe, as I devour a saucer of them by the fire. Alas, my many cats may not partake in them, and I must turn deaf ears to their pleas. Though this recipe calls for their favorite fish, its preparation requires exotic seasonings, salts and spices noxious to their delicate feline constitutions. I wonder if they understand my explanations when I deny them this delicious snack. For the cat is cryptic, and lately their conversations seem to have a conspiratorial air, as if they were plotting to overpower me in my sleep and make me their dinner. Well, a cat worshiper like myself should aspire proudly to such consumption. A true apotheosis, the ultimate communion between feline and man. Perhaps tonight.

THE SPIRALING MADNESS OF BAAR'BEK-HU

Spiral barbecue chips, no one can eat just Juan.

SERVES 6 TO 8
PREP TIME: 10 MINUTES   **TOTAL TIME:** 20 MINUTES

THE LURE

4 russet potatoes

I teaspoon brown sugar

½ teaspoon black peppercorns

½ teaspoon cayenne pepper

½ teaspoon celery salt

½ teaspoon garlic powder

½ teaspoon grains of paradise, whole

½ teaspoon ground cinnamon

½ teaspoon mustard power

½ teaspoon onion powder

½ teaspoon salt

½ teaspoon smoked paprika

Oil for frying

SPRING THE TRAP

◎ With a vegetable brush, baptize the tubers under cold, running water. Flay each of them. Drown them in cold water until ready to cut.

◎ Spiralize them or cut them thusly. Impale the offering from the narrow end to the other. With a small sharp blade, cut into the narrow end until metal touches wood. Rotate the potato slowly to make thin slices, leaving a spiraling cut through the tuber along the skewer. When you have reached the end, slide the thus lacerated offering down the skewer.

◎ Soak the potato spirals in water for 30 minutes.

◎ While the potato spirals are soaking, use a spice grinder or mortar and pestle to grind all the spices to a fine barbecue powder.

◎ With paper towels, pat the potato spirals completely dry.

◎ If left intact, fry the potatoes one at a time or, if cut into chips, fry in batches until crispy. Don't overcrowd the chips in the oil.

◎ Remove the potatoes from oil onto a wire rack or paper towel. Dust with barbecue seasoning immediately.

◎ Serve by themselves or with Double Bockrug's Cauldron (page 179).

Chips within chips in a spiral array...

The sequence and the curvature are all important. If there is any gap larger than their limbs or heads, they will be upon you. The words must be written into the surface as I have written them here. They must spin and turn and never stop, or they will be upon you.

If you have come this far, learned this much, it is too late. These spiral fragments are your only hope. You must obtain the correct seasons to tempt them into the trap, or they will be upon you.

The oil is important as well. It turns the blades with silence. If there is noise, someone will investigate. Eventually someone will interfere, and they will be upon you. You must find an isolated place to entrap them. It must be a place no one will disturb for a long while, longer than your life if possible. They are unerring. They will find you over any distance, in any era, through any dimension, and past any ward. I have sought a region with no angles, a plane with no edge. I am close, but I have had to use these traps many times now when each attempt has failed. The more I travel the ultrarealms, the more I attract their ire, and the more issue forth from those nightmare corkscrew towers. Someday it will be too many. Someday they will come when I am asleep or helpless, and they will be upon me.

—written on sheets of paper cut in concentric spirals, found in the attic of an abandoned house, Providence, Rhode Island, 1937

[According to police reports dated a few months after the notations in a grimoire—the stolen property of Miskatonic University—the resident disappeared that same year. Odd claw marks matching no-known canid or any local fauna appeared in profusion along floor, walls, and ceiling. A silver vegetable peeler engraved with odd characters lay near a sack of what presumably had been potatoes.]

THE BITTER BLEND

AMOS TRUFFLES

A dark treat for those who treat with darkness

SERVES 6 TO 8
PREP TIME: 10 MINUTES   **TOTAL TIME:** 8 HOURS 20 MINUTES

HIS DARK MATERIALS

4 ounces bitter beer

2 tablespoons heavy cream

6 ounces 70 to 80 percent dark chocolate

100 percent cocoa powder

TRUFFLE BREWING

◉ In a small saucepan over low heat, simmer the beer until it reduces by half.

◉ Add the cream, stir well, and simmer for 2 to 3 minutes. Turn off the heat.

◉ Break the chocolate into small chunks and put them in a metal bowl.

◉ Using a double boiler or other means, slowly melt the dark chocolate.

◉ When the chocolate has melted fully, add the beer-cream mixture. It will look awful, but keep stirring until it fully intermingles.

◉ Allow the hideous mixture to cool to room temperature, cover, and refrigerate overnight.

◉ With a melon baller or small spoon, scoop 1-inch balls from the bowl.

◉ Roll the spheres in the cocoa powder until fully covered and arrange them on a white plate, keeping them refrigerated until serving.

It is said that, in days gone, the messengers of the Great Ones kept a container of these on hand to pacify the various guard beasts and servitor minions along their routes.

Do not feed to earthly pets.

Appease guests of all walks, orders, dimensionalities, and forms of matter.

Damn that Haddon! At first, the trove he brought from the wretched Tuttles' estate elated me, but how I wish I'd never seen those books or that seemingly innocent inclusion among them. It was no more than a simple recipe for a sweet snack or dessert—or so it seemed.

The instructions stood sandwiched between the R'lyeh Text and The Necronomicon. That such rare, exquisite volumes had been allowed to touch the cheap notepaper of this recipe left me aghast. I expected it to have detached from one of the other tomes, but relief came when that proved not to be the case. Still, from the beginning, I felt compelled to examine it and understand it in detail. I must have stared blankly at the page in my hand for several moments before I realized that its language was plain, not related at all to some hokey religion or ancient spell. Worse, once I understood it, I had to attempt it. My hands shook with the need to busy themselves in the library's small galley. How it came to be stocked with precisely what I needed I dare not guess.

Had I imagined phantasmal pounding footsteps as I reduced the chocolate block? Surely it was nothing more than the sound of pestle against bowl on the stout preparation table. Less could I be forgiven for assigning them to the rolling simmer, and how I continued to delude myself when scooping them from the bowl. Such is not the functioning of a sane mind.

I arranged them, complete, on a serving plate—for whom, I cannot say. They seemed to prefer a nested pyramidal design. Yes, I know how that sounds. But with each judder of the ground beneath campus, they slowly deranged into that other sigil. My mind recoiled to behold it and reckon what colossal hideousness it signified.

They cannot reach the final configuration. Aylesbury Road must not be repeated! Not here, not in my beloved and hallowed halls! They will find me here in the morning, for there is no time to awaken enough souls willing to share the burden. They will find me here, bloated and raving, but the plate will stand empty. Even the paper that bore this cursed "treat" shall I have devoured.

—last entry before incarceration, diary of Dr. Llanfer,
head librarian of Miskatonic University

BYAQUICHE

Get carried away by this stellar pepper and onion quiche.

SERVES 6
PREP TIME: 4 HOURS 20 MINUTES   **TOTAL TIME:** 6 HOURS

PROVISIONS

I large bunch Swiss chard
I red onion
½ red bell pepper
½ green bell pepper
½ yellow bell pepper
2 garlic cloves
Olive oil for sautéing
I teaspoon salt
½ teaspoon freshly ground black
   pepper
½ teaspoon ground nutmeg
I teaspoon sweet paprika
I teaspoon garlic powder

THE CRUST-ACEAN SHELL

1¼ cups all-purpose flour, plus
   more for dusting
½ teaspoon salt
½ teaspoon granulated sugar
I large egg
I teaspoon bacon fat or lard
8 tablespoons (I stick) unsalted
   butter, cold, plus more at room
   temperature for greasing

SUMMON THE BYAQUICHE

◉ Blanch, rinse, dry, and chop the Swiss chard.

◉ Medium dice the red onion, dice the bell pepper, and mince the garlic.

◉ In a large frying pan over medium-high heat, add a glug of olive oil and sauté the garlic for 2 minutes.

◉ Add the chard and stir for a couple of minutes. Remove from the pan and set aside.

◉ In the same pan, over medium heat and with some more oil, sauté the onion and peppers for 4 to 5 minutes, until they soften.

◉ Add the sautéed chard back to the pan and season with the salt, pepper, nutmeg, paprika, and garlic powder. Stir for 2 to 3 minutes until fully incorporated.

◉ Transfer to a bowl and refrigerate for at least 3 hours. Remove 1 hour before building the quiche.

◉ Next create the shell. Combine the flour, salt, and sugar, and sift them together into a medium bowl.

◉ Add the egg and bacon fat to the center of the dry ingredients. Mix by hand until fully combined.

◉ Cut the cold butter into small cubes and add it to the dough.

◉ Add ⅛ to ¼ cup cold water, little by little, as you thoroughly mix the dough. Knead it into a smooth ball.

◉ Wrap the dough in plastic and refrigerate for 30 minutes to 1 hour.

CONTINUES

The key, I'm told, is to lean forward and bring your heels up behind you, otherwise the wing membrane will keep hitting your feet!

Even in space they'll occasionally flap those smelly wings, and I've no idea why!

They truly are foul beasts, these byakhee. Consuming what the handlers have come to call the Byaquiche, along with a flagon of special mead, calms the mind and stomache, preventing the fast travel sickness.

It does nothing, however, to help with the Byakhee stench!

YELLOW MATTER CUSTARD

2 large eggs, plus 1 egg yolk

⅓ cup Parmesan, Romano, or other hard cheese of choice

⅓ cup Gruyère or similar

⅓ cup heavy cream

⅛ to ¼ cup whole milk

① Preheat the oven to 350°F.

① Remove the dough from the fridge and, with a floured rolling pin, roll it into a 14-inch disk.

① Butter the bottom and sides of a quiche pan.

① Transfer the dough disk into the pan, press it against the sides of the pan, and poke the bottom all over with a fork to avoid the creation of space-time bubbles.

① Bake the shell for 10 to 12 minutes, until the bottom firms. Remove and let cool.

① While the crust is cooling, create the custard. In a small bowl, beat the eggs and yolk.

① In a medium bowl, grate both pieces of cheese.

① Add the cream and beaten eggs to the grated cheese and mix.

① Add milk in small amounts, while mixing, until the custard becomes pourable.

① Set the prebaked crust on a baking sheet. Add spoonfuls of the bitter filling to cover the bottom.

① Pour the custard all over the filling, spreading it evenly.

① Bake at 350°F for 10 to 15 minutes, checking frequently, until the shell turns golden and the custard begins to burn a little.

① Serve warm.

Fly by Fright, Part II

Our guide's choice of path didn't enthuse us, but the Byakhee would have come out of its nest if Carstairs had succeeded with the ritual described in the last issue. As it happened, either the whistle and chant did work, or the thing just happened to be away. In any case, we captured an egg! A horrible, mottled thing, it has an earthy, somewhat bitter, rather enticing aroma. We spied a human arm in the nest and evidence of prior meals less easily identifiable but no less mammalian, so we didn't tarry.

With our fragile burden, the climb down proved arduous. We alternated scanning the rocks below for holds and the skies above for returning mother horrors. We've no idea if the Weatherby would prove any use against such a thing, and we did not want to find out while clinging to a cliff face. Our parkas and packs bore every variation of the Elder Sign we could discover, and we hoped them sufficient and effective. Judging by the size of the egg, these monstrosities must be larger than horses. Luckily, we never did get a close look. At one point, a dark, winged shape appeared on the horizon and gave us quite the fright. In truth, it did not seem like any bird that any of us ever had seen. Thank the Nameless that it came no closer.

We happily left Bihar, hoping greatly that the beasts had no faculty for tracking their spawn. As the journey home proved uneventful, we made many measurements and notes regarding our prize. Carstairs rejoined us en route, in the middle of the North Atlantic. A woman on the upper deck raved insensibly about a huge bird that dropped a man. Carstairs got drunk on the mead required for the journey, which I suspect had something to do with his dramatic choice of return.

We know the ritual works, and the things can be put safely to use. Carstairs may be as reckless as he is brave, but we could not have succeeded without him. We only had to convince the crew that he accompanied us when we disembarked and to keep him from using the egg in a recipe he had been on about until morning. Either the mead or the travel modality left him quite famished. I was glad when he finally fell asleep, as I myself could wait no longer for breakfast, after spending days eating the fare of our hosts.

We none of us are eager to visit Leng again.

—from *The Unnaturalist*, Issue 14, September 1928

CRAISIN DREAMS

Nightmarishly good lemon-craisin bars

SERVES 8 TO 10
TOTAL TIME: 45 MINUTES

THE LOGIC

Unsalted butter or nonstick cooking spray for greasing

1 cup frozen lemonade concentrate, thawed

1 cup granulated sugar

8 tablespoons (1 stick) unsalted butter

2 eggs

3 cups all-purpose flour

1½ tablespoons grated lemon peel

1 teaspoon baking soda

1 teaspoon salt

1 cup (or more) dried cranberries

SINK INTO THE DREAMSCAPE

0 Preheat the oven to 375°F.

0 Grease a baking pan with butter or cooking spray.

0 In a medium bowl, combine the lemonade concentrate, sugar, butter, and eggs. Mix well.

0 Add the flour, lemon peel, baking soda, and salt and stir well.

0 Stir in the cranberries and pour the batter into the baking pan.

0 Bake for 30 minutes, until light brown.

0 Allow the Dreams to cool to room temperature.

0 With a cookie cutter or by hand, cut the dreams into desired shapes. If you can't find a skull-shaped cutter, an inverted snowman, when stretched a bit, makes a nice skull shape in a pinch.

They came to me in a dream. There were many crawling over each other towards me. Their exposed skulls were sickeningly soft and spongy and were pitted with holes. Of mouths or noses, they had none, but had what seemed to be numerous lidless eyes, some which bulged or hung from the surface, some which lay recessed in the sunken face holes.

You needn't be careful of how the various eyes are arranged upon the heads.

I see them. I close my eyes, and I see them. They used to come only in dreams. Now they are simply there, behind my eyes. They're skulls. Their skulls . . . are spongiform. I fear mine is becoming like them. I don't know. I . . . have no extra eyes. They have many: red, dully translucent, staring, daring, daring me to look away, to nourish myself with something other than their effigies.

I hunger for them. I wake, needing their soft velvety texture, and their sharp bite. I bite them. They bite me. My belly is full, but I reach for another. I feel their gaze from the tray, waiting. I sink my teeth into their soft skulls, one after another.

In dream, they walk on ghostly legs with no shape. Awake, they float before me if I so much as blink. It is time to make more.

Today, I will take them to the blue fortress of metal and glass. I will share them. The Doctor will be pleased. My dream bars will bring him more patients. The snickering secretary will be the first to fall. I'll show her the red staring eyes, and she will be delighted to partake. The One Behind Glass, the One of Ten Thousand Steps, he, too, will bend. He will partake—even as he sneers at me. To each floor will I go, my trays a gift unwanted—at first.

The next day, I will bring more, and the third day, they will be waiting for me, waiting for the doors to open and the dreams to begin.

I see them. They, too, will see them, and they will look back.

—transcript of hypnotherapy session 4, Patient 116

Clinician's Notes: Session ends. Patient became unresponsive when, again, denied access to the kitchen. Scrawled some kind of recipe on the two-way mirror. Perhaps I'll ask Margaret to try it out when I get home. Patient 116's reaction may be instructive if I have a tray to share tomorrow.

DISCS OF WASA'BI

Strange delicacies from the king of Prussia

MAKES APPROXIMATELY 80 COOKIES
PREP TIME: 1 HOUR 15 MINUTES   **TOTAL TIME:** 1 HOUR 30 MINUTES

PETITION

6 tablespoons (¾ stick) unsalted
    butter, room temperature

⅜ cup coconut oil

½ cup granulated sugar

½ cup brown sugar

1 teaspoon low-sodium soy sauce

2 eggs

2½ tablespoons ground ginger

1¼ teaspoons baking soda

1¼ cups all-purpose flour

½ cup wasabi peas

COMMANDMENTS

⓪ With a stand mixer, cream the butter, coconut oil, and sugars until well blended.

⓪ One at a time, add 1 egg, the soy sauce, ginger, baking soda, and flour to create a sticky dough. Refrigerate the dough for 1 hour.

⓪ Preheat the oven to 350°F.

⓪ Separate the remaining egg and reserve the egg white for the glaze. Use the yolk for Arthur Jermyn's Chocolate Banana Bread (page 44), the Snacks of Ulthar (page 148), or Byaquiche (page 159).

⓪ Into a 1-gallon plastic freezer bag, add the wasabi peas. Seal the bag and, using a rolling pin, crush the peas into a coarse powder.

⓪ Line a baking sheet with parchment paper.

⓪ Remove ¼ of the dough at a time, leaving the rest in the refrigerator to retain firmness, and form it into teaspoon-size balls.

⓪ Place the balls on the parchment paper, about 2 inches apart.

⓪ Flatten the dough balls and glaze with the egg white.

⓪ Generously sprinkle with the crushed wasabi peas.

⓪ Bake for 9 to 10 minutes for a bitter, crispy, chewy cookie.

Two opposed flavors
in harmonious balance.
Unexpected.

These do not
last long.
Perhaps that
is why he made
so many.

And so
should you.

O Great Wasa'bi, long have we awaited your return. You who lend your burning fire to the devout and deserving, forever will you reign over the roots of civilization. Into all nations, you will nourish the taste for your sacred fire. Foretold it is even that beverages will be concocted in your honor to venerate and assuage He Who Is Not to Be Named. Such is your power, O Great Green One!

By artifice of these discs, we send your reach farther. We place them as sacramental wafers in the mouths of the uninitiated. As familiar as they are in form, so will they be novel in flavor. Those who seek experience, even at bitter cost, will savor the offering. The courageous will flock to your banner, while the weak will be consumed with burning.

The spheres carry your potency, and they will be loosed to batter even as they shatter and sink into the harmonious joining of opposites. Iä! Iä Wasa'bi

[indecipherable]

Armies of powerful spirits will rise to your aid. Your word will take root in distant places. Great will be your crop. Legends will awaken in the minds of those touched by your power. The winds will carry the sacred scent. Even to the Kitchens of Furthest Night will your aroma reach! They will seek and crave you in all the Ten Thousand Things. With this and the other libations and sacraments foretold will you be known in heretofore unforeseen pairings.

The discs carry your blessing: discs upon discs upon discs. These will be carried by hands and fly like the chariot wheels of the Sky Ones of old. Ancient you are, but new joy will you be to whom the disks fly. You who fly upon the Wind, grown from the Earth, formed in Water, and bearer of Fire, you, Great Wasa'bi, are nigh! Iä! Iä!

Tongues will speak your name, even as your power enfolds them. Iä Wasa'bi! Iä Wasa'bi fhtagn!

—scroll found in archives of the Prussian Court of [redacted], translation incomplete and unvalidated, likely imperfect given the strange dialect and atypical characters.

JNSANI-TEA BISCUITS

Maddeningly tart chocolate-cherry scones

MAKES 16
PREP TIME: I HOUR   **TOTAL TIME:** I HOUR 20 MINUTES

HALLUCINATIONS

¾ cup whole milk

¼ cup loose the Earl in Grey tea
(or Earl Grey of choice), plus
2 teaspoons

⅓ cup dried tart cherries

12 tablespoons (I½ sticks)
unsalted butter, cold, plus
more at room temperature for
greasing

3 cups all-purpose flour, plus
more for dusting

5 teaspoons baking powder

¾ teaspoon salt

½ teaspoon freshly ground black
pepper

½ cup brown sugar, packed

I egg

⅓ cup dark chocolate chips

THE GLAZED LOOK

2 cups powdered sugar

2 tablespoons whole milk

I teaspoon vanilla extract

I teaspoon lemon extract

3 drops yellow food coloring

THE ACTS

◐ In a saucepan over low heat, add the milk.

◐ When the milk has warmed, add ¼ cup of loose the Earl in Grey tea. Brew for 10 minutes. Strain the milk and refrigerate.

◐ In 1 cup of boiling-hot water, brew 2 teaspoons of loose the Earl in Grey tea for 5 minutes.

◐ Strain the tea into a bowl and add the dried cherries. Cover and allow the cherries to infuse for at least 10 minutes.

◐ Preheat the oven to 400°F and lightly grease two baking sheets.

◐ In a large bowl or stand mixer, combine the flour, baking powder, salt, and pepper.

◐ Add the sugar and mix well to combine.

◐ Cut the butter into small chunks and mix by hand into the dry ingredients. The dough should be crumbly.

◐ Add the egg and, by hand or with a stand mixer fitted with a paddle, mix well.

◐ Slowly add the tea milk to the mix and combine well.

◐ Drain the infused cherries. Add the cherries and the chocolate chips to the dough and mix well. If the dough is too wet, slowly add a little flour and mix to desired consistency.

◐ On a lightly floured surface, turn the dough out and knead gently. If still too wet, add flour as needed. Roll the dough out, and fold over a few times.

CONTINUES

0 Roll the dough out into a 6-inch circle and cut it in half. Roll the halves out, folding them over a few times, and then each into a 6-inch circle. Both circles should have a uniform thickness.

0 Cut the two dough disks into asymmetrical eighths and place on the baking sheets.

0 Bake for 20 to 22 minutes, until the scones have a nice golden-brown top.

0 Allow them to cool to room temperature before glazing.

0 In a medium bowl, whisk together the powdered sugar, milk, extracts, and food coloring, adding up to 2 additional teaspoons of milk for desired consistency.

0 Drizzle the glaze over the scones.

If he looks up, he will see me. Even from the street below, he will see me. He will see that the scones are fewer. He will see the kettle is nearly empty now. His knowing gaze and the smile on his puffy white lips tell me that he knows there is tea inside the biscuits!

He is not the Earl. He is a harbinger, a servant, a spy. The recipe is come by honestly. Only did I pray for a tea of this character, and by the same agency it was delivered, was the recipe for the accompanying biscuits transmitted. Kettiel is his name, and he is the Angel given dominion over such things. Such a one could have no truck with the Earl, nor the King. No, they are wroth that I have been gifted thus. They send their grub to bedevil me. I shall paint him as he really is and not the face he shows. He is from the churchyard but not the portion that sees the light of the sun.

There is not time. I cannot reach the papers with this knowledge and convince the haughty type-men to tell my tale. I record it here, with the sharpened edge of my argent teaspoon. I write what to use and how to prepare them in the oak itself. No stray wind will snare a page from my dead hand. Let them try to take the table through the window!

Have you seen the Yellow Glaze? [burned into the wood, in a different hand]

There! Proof! These are not my words! An acrid whiff of woodsmoke as I finished the portrait of the watchman, and here I find this damnable question again! He mouths it to me as he stares up from his churchyard. He is too horrible to behold, and I know he is here for me. The time is short. My fingers ache from my labor. The pot is empty. My cup is empty. The plate is empty. My palette is empty. My jars are empty. My canvas is empty! Empty! Heaven grant that these words carved into the sacred wood with the holy metal withstand the plot of the King in Yellow and his grey minion, the earl.

O priest, I wish you to send my body away. Bury it anywhere but in that churchyard! With the dregs of the tea, I anoint my forehead with the—

—carving found in a table near a window in a New York City apartment;
tenant's body discovered with two others

SESAME SIGIL SPREAD

A gore-may wasabi-cream cheese Thing you really . . . dig.

SERVES BECOMES 8 TO 10 PEOPLE
TOTAL TIME: 5 MINUTES

WHAT WILL BE CONJOINED

One 8-ounce package cream
  cheese
Wasabi paste
Sesame seeds
Soy sauce

THE HIDEOLICIOUS AMALGAMATIONI

① Bisect the cream cheese lengthwise and spread a layer of wasabi paste over the top of the bottom half.

① Generously sprinkle sesame seeds atop the wasabi paste, then cover with the top half of the bar.

① Carve cream cheese into desired shape, then douse the top with soy sauce so it pools at the bottom. You can use silicone molds for the top if frozen for a few hours. (The cream cheese quickly regains its pliability once out of the mold, almost like it's alive.) If you use a mold, shape the bottom half roughly the same size and shape.

It makes no sense. These slabs of material came from Philadelphia. How did they get to Japan? Why are they so heavy yet so pliable? Were they always alabaster white? We know what buildings they came from, just not how. That awful visage, that was never carved on the face of either of the damaged edifices. The Japanese have a better handle on the greenish substance oozing from between the slabs. As for the oblong objects adhering to the top, I swear I heard one of our colleagues say, "Sesame." I thought he was joking, like those crazy runes translated to "open sesame" or something, but they do look like giant— No, that's just nuts.

Their chemist distinctly mentioned "Kikko" or "Kikko men." I don't know what that means. It's their site; if they want to have little jokes, sure, whatever. I wish my Japanese was better. I could be of more help.

They keep asking about dairy products from back home. There are tiny scoops from the main slabs, running through the green goop, so many of them. When I got back from lunch, nobody else seemed to have gone yet, and they didn't seem hungry. Oh well, their loss. I guess it's just the usual fare to them, but I love the cuisine here.

Got some of that stuff in my eye. Hot damn, it burned! I thought I was going to lose my eye. The site doc looked me over and laughed. Something about "never touch your face." Maybe I should get some goggles.

Today a thin brown liquid, very runny, started leaking from somewhere up top. Definitely getting those goggles. The local team was very excited. I could make out little of their conversation, and no one wanted to explain. Something about "final piece" or "missing ingredient." They don't have much use for me since we solved the Philadelphia part of the puzzle, and I don't understand what's going on. I hope the boss is happy with whatever I managed to contribute. DoD is going to want to know what softens building facades and moves them to the other side of the planet, but that's way above my pay grade. I'm not even going to let on that's a possibility. As far as I'm concerned, this is some cross-cultural architectural project. I just don't know from what cult—ure that relief in the top slab comes.

I have to get out of here. Today I found rice cracker fragments embedded in the object. They match the shape of those tiny sample troughs I found earlier. I know they noticed. I tried to pretend I hadn't seen anything. They're eating it! I'm going to pack up now. Great visit, but it's time for this Philly boy to go. I'm in way over my head. I may not mention this part. Smile, wave—get to the airport.

—field notes, US Geological Survey International Cooperative

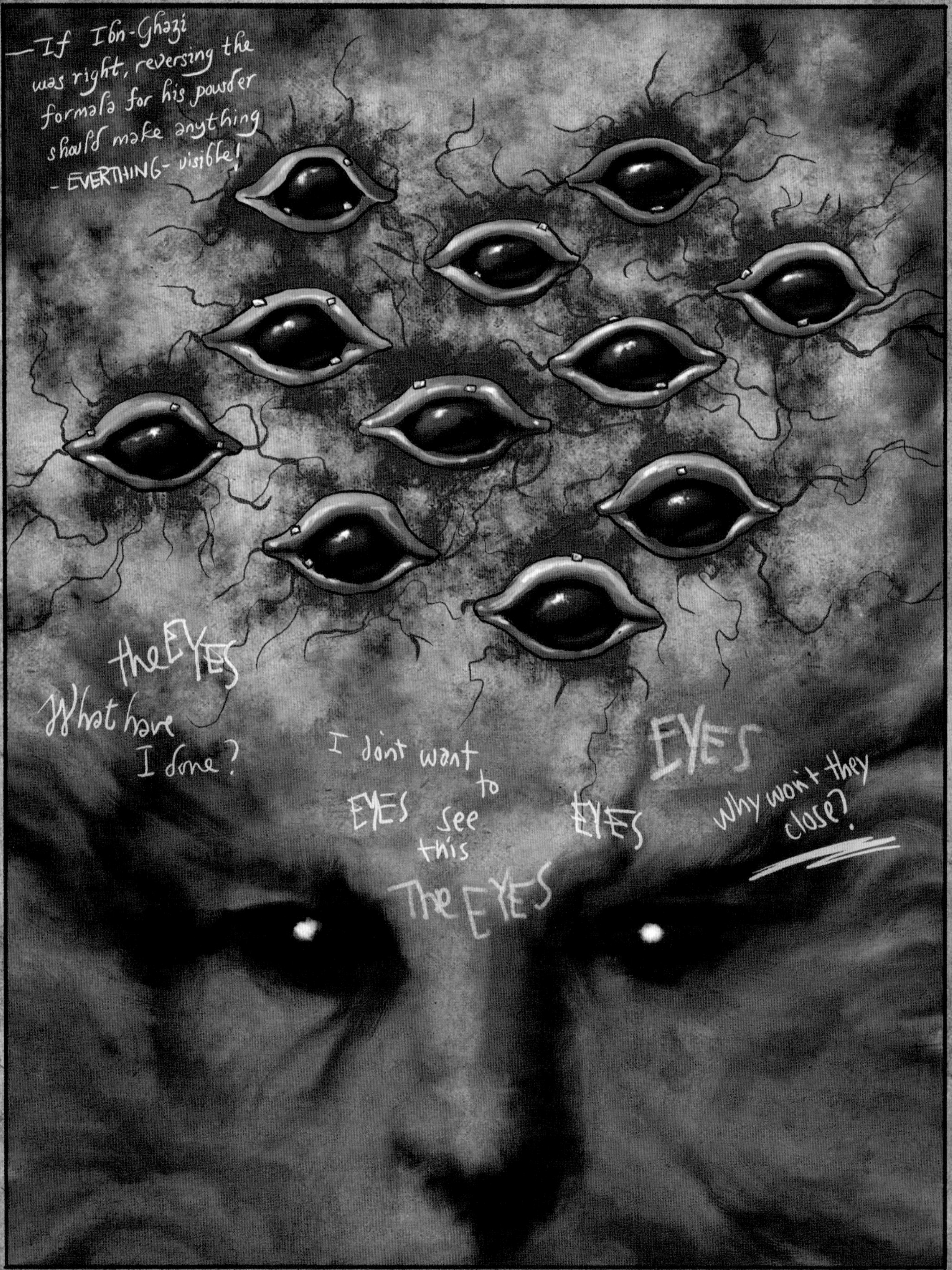
—If Ibn-Ghazi was right, reversing the formula for his powder should make anything - EVERTHING- visible!
the EYES
What have I done?
I dont want to see this
EYES
The EYES
EYES
EYES
why won't they close?

THE UNBLINKING EYES

Visions of caramel-wrapped chocolate coffee beans with a synergistic kick

---

YIELDS 60 EYES
PREP TIME: 10 MINUTES **TOTAL TIME:** 30 MINUTES

OPTICAL PROFUSIONS

Cayenne pepper, finely ground

Sea salt, coarse

6 ounces caramels (about 20 Kraft caramels)

60 milk or dark chocolate–covered coffee beans

EYEBALL IT

◉ Red-eye, set, go! In a small bowl, add the cayenne pepper.

◉ Line a baking sheet with parchment paper and sprinkle the sea salt across it.

◉ Melt the caramel, taking care not to burn it, via the twice-boiling cauldron or in four 10-second bursts, on high in the small wave chamber, until very soft.

◉ When the caramel cools enough to handle but remains pliable, pinch a dollop about twice the size of a coffee bean, roll it into a ball, then flatten it into a disk.

◉ Dust the caramel disk with cayenne pepper and wrap it around a coffee bean. (Find courage and trust; this is a key ingredient!).

◉ Pinch the ends to make an eye-shape and set the unblinking eye on the salt.

◉ Repeat, working quickly, and reheating the remaining caramel in 10 second bursts if needed to keep it pliant. Don't burn your fingers. The caramel is hot, and it sticks, which we may have learned the hard way. Heed our warning!

◉ Let the eyes gaze cooly to room temperature before serving.

Powder. So try a whole? Perhaps several. Come up with a way to control the dosage.

For ten heartbeats. No, won't do. Needs to be stronger. Add two stimulants and something to prolong the effect. Sugar?

I want to see all of it. Must find a catalyst that accomplishes the revelation all at once. Something that hits by surprise and opens the eyes—all of them—at once. Ibn-Ghazi was blundering around in the dark with his "alchemy." Magic! Indeed. I shall surpass him, though he did obtain results that pointed the way. Must give him that. Something from the bayou perhaps. Where is that red phial?

Yes, these or several of them should be enough to induce the right vibrational state! They even look a bit like eyes that cannot close. Ha! Yes, what was it Fuller said? "It is not beautiful when there is nothing more to add but rather when there is nothing else to take away." Something like that. He'd agree with their simple effectiveness. No need for embellishment.

This formulation is definitely better than the one without the catalyst. Counterintuitive but, like so much else, it must be experienced to be understood.

Dosage testing: One or two at my weight and resistance are enjoyable but produce no noticeable effects. Four and I begin to feel the senses sharpen. Note: they are not taken all at once or in rapid succession but leisurely. Perhaps I'll just make a large batch and leave them out for casual ingestion.

The eyes are vibrating. I'm not sure which, them or mine. I've lost count and had too many. Damnably poppable. One doesn't even notice oneself reaching for the bowl until the tremors become pronounced. The shakes become a warning. This will have to run its course.

I see them! THEM! They are HERE! ALL AROUND! Even with my eyes clenched shut, they exist in the space between pupil and lid! There is no escape. None! Yes. One. One escape.

[red smudge]

—transcription from pocket recorder found in Tillinghast laboratory

DOUBLE BOCKRUG'S CAULDRON

From depths rise a double bock beer and sharp, seasoned Cheddar.

SERVES 6 TO 10
PREP TIME: 10 MINUTES   **TOTAL TIME:** 25 MINUTES

DREDGED PRESENCE

2 to 3 green onions or scallions

4 to 6 strips bacon, cooked

1 bottle double bock (doppelbock) beer, room temperature

6 cups (1½ pounds) shredded sharp Cheddar

BOKRUG'S DARK GIFT

❶ Finely chop the onions and bacon.

❷ To a large pot, add the onions and beer and simmer for 15 to 20 minutes. Do not let it boil.

❸ Add the bacon and stir gently.

❹ Slowly add ¼ cup of cheese at a time, gently stirring until all the cheese melts and fully liquifies. Slowly raise the heat to medium as you go. Take care not to scald or burn the mixture. Continue stirring the cheese, like a restless god slumbering on a lake bottom, until you've added it all and the mixture has a uniform texture.

❺ Serve hot with peeled and scored cucumber slices, your favorite veggies, or chips.

❻ The Water-Lizard will be pleased.

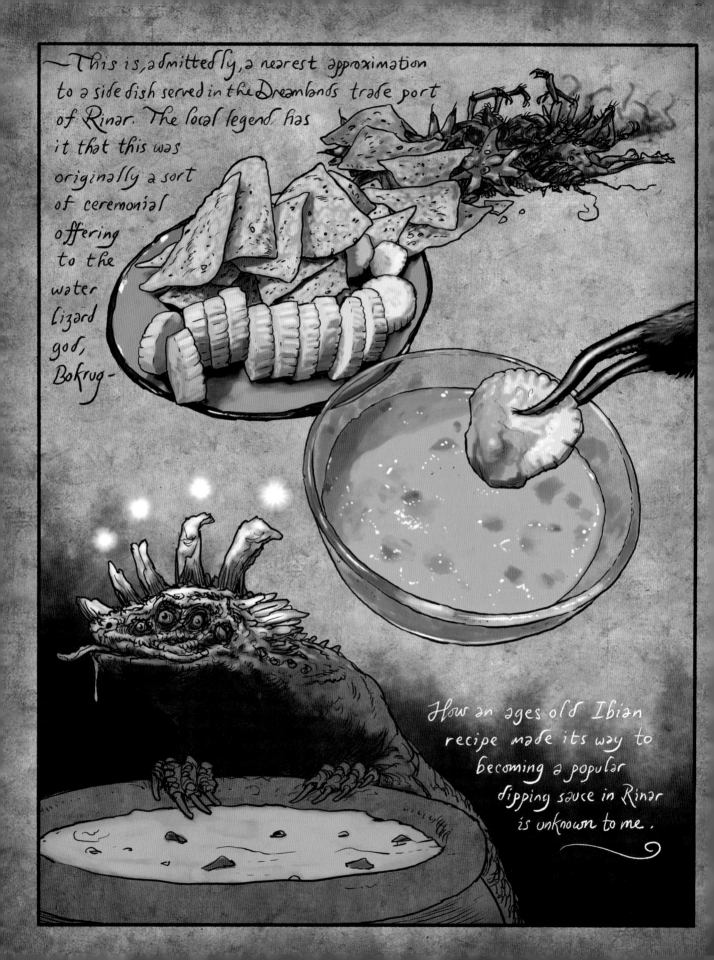

—This is, admittedly, a nearest approximation to a side dish served in the Dreamlands trade port of Rinar. The local legend has it that this was originally a sort of ceremonial offering to the water lizard god, Bokrug—

How an ages old Ibian recipe made its way to becoming a popular dipping sauce in Rinar is unknown to me.

The people of IBU were brought low, My cherished, destroyed. Their unmakers reveled in their deed. They stole My likeness, chiseled in sea-green beryl, for their priests to conduct hopeless rituals in execration of My memory. Each year, their affront to Me grew in fervor and outrageous extravagance. Upon My shores, they repeated in effigy unspeakable acts committed upon the innocent and delighted in their depraved acts of murder and desecration.

Unwary and innocent were My people when they fell upon them, and so did I let 1,000 passings of this orb around its sun expire so that they might forget the meaning of their celebration, rise to prosperity, and then be thrown down in a single night, as their forebears did to their placid and benignant neighbors. My feast equaled their thousand feasts. Their screams echoed those of the people of IBU, for I opened time and let them commingle as I slaughtered them. My lake turned thick with their gore as My claws raked and scored their nobles before I flayed them, dipping them all in the sea of turgid succulence that I had made. This will be the new commemoration. Each year, Bokrug will have the double feast, and under the moon whence We came will the damned contest with one another again. Each year on this day, the lake will become dark and thick with the lives of Man and the flesh of the Cherished. Such is My will, and they who wish to remember will do so in fear of My wrath!

—transcript from psychic sensitive allegedly channeling "Bokrug" through a stone cylinder recovered from an unknown estate, 1928

Clinicians' Notes: Possessed of great strength and determination, the "psychic" wouldn't release the artifact after the session, carrying it with him into the kitchen, where he ransacked the larders and bar to unknown purpose. We saw no credible harm in letting his fit run its course and relented in our attempts to subdue him without injury or risk of damage to the cylinder. Eventually he produced a singularly enjoyable pot of fondue, which we relished equally with fresh vegetables and chips. He absolutely refused to relinquish the artefact until every one of us had tried his concoction. It seemed a small price to pay to regain such a precious relic without harm or further incident. I hope Emmy got that down in her notes. I'm going to have to make it for bridge night next week!

THE FLATS OF ULTHAR

When you stare at the Abyssinian, the Abyssinian stares back.

SERVES 4 WHO DREAM OR RUN WILD AT 3 AM FOR NO DISCERNIBLE REASON
PREP TIME: 10 MINUTES **TOTAL TIME:** 35 MINUTES

PICK OF THE LITTER

4 corn tortillas

2 tablespoons neutral oil, such as corn

1 tablespoon lime juice

Chili powder

Coarse sea salt

1 cup raw pepitas (pumpkin seeds) or sunflower seeds

2 plum tomatoes

1 jalapeño pepper

½ yellow onion

3 tablespoons chopped cilantro

PLAY TIME!

0 Preheat the oven to 350°F.

0 Cut tortillas into kitty or paw shapes and place on a baking sheet.

0 In a small bowl, whisk together the oil and lime juice and brush it onto the tortilla pieces.

0 Sprinkle with chili powder and sea salt to taste.

0 Bake for 8 to 10 minutes, until crisp.

0 While the tortillas are baking, toast the pepitas in a dry frying pan over medium heat.

0 Process the toasted pepitas coarsely in the food scary thing that makes lots of noise. (We'll be under the bed until you're done.)

0 In the hot dry frying pan or on a grill, char the tomatoes, pepper, and onion until they blister and scorch. For milder heat, remove the ribs and seeds from the pepper.

0 To the noise maker, add the charred vegetables, cilantro, pepitas, and salt to taste and grind to a smooth paste. (See you next Tuesday.)

0 Make sounds indicating that you're pleased with yourself and go play with your food.

It is wise to be kind to them.

[Elderly woman bends over to place something on the ground outside a cottage. Shapes of cats move at the edge of the adjoining field.]

WOMAN: Oh yes, we feed the cats every night and make sure they have fresh water or, if times are good, milk.

REPORTER: So there's a colony of ferals here. How many?

WOMAN: No, there's no problem with the strays. They're not even here during the day. They come only at night if the moon is out. But if Saturn's visible, best not to be near anything that looks like a cat. We still leave food and water, but we don't visit with those ones.

[A cat so white it seems to be glowing in the moonlight approaches with a bouncing stride and tail raised in a question mark.]

Oh, here comes Pepito! He's so nice. Yes, he's friendly. See, he rubs your leg. Yes, you should pet him. These cats don't give the allergies, only the misfortune they want you to have or avoid. I put his favorite salsa down. He can't be hurt by anything from here, like a regular cat. You and your allergies! Did your mother never let you make mud pies? I bet you wash your hands so much they bleed.

[More cats approach seemingly from the night air.]

REPORTER: How long have you been feeding them like this? Do you always stay and spend time with each one?

WOMAN: A hundred years or more. If I stop, I may as well just crawl into my grave.

[She laughs. A camera glitch makes the distant tree line visible through her for a moment.]

REPORTER: We didn't see a single cat here while we set up. We wondered if you were just a legend.

[The camera sweeps the ground, showing the reporter up to his calves in purring cats. The woman produces a basket of tortillas and salsa paste to share. The reporter and cats share a late-night snack.]

—transcript of local interest piece broadcast by KATT 104,
Aragon, New Mexico, 1947

AKLO-KNOWLEDG-MEATS

In the end, all was darkness, and . . . er, I mean. From the beginning, we've been blessed to work with incredible, awesome people. If you've been with us since then and know *The Necronomnomnom* and *LoveCraft Cocktails*, you'll have seen some of these names before. I'm going to thank them again because they grow more awesome with time. We have a few new friends to thank as well!

Firstly, Miguel Fliguer is a joy to work with. Not only have we written several stories together, but now we also have hashed out more than a few recipes together. For the first time in the pages of a Nom-iverse book, you can enjoy his magnificent writing chops, too. He brought us: Amos Truffles (recipe); Arthur Jermyn's Chocolate-Banana Bread; Brownie Jenkin (story); Byaquiche (recipe); Dunwich Whipoorwings; The Gateau and the Key Lime; Hen-Thai Corn Tacos; Innsmouth Roe (with thanks again to wife Myriam for the alchemical assistance); Innsmouthfuls (story); KALEM Club Sandwiches; Lemonic Pozestion; Morguearita Slabs (story); The Sign of Knish (story in collaboration with Mike and recipe crafted and perfected over the years by wife, Myriam); the Snacks of Ulthar; Ubbo-Salsa (story in collaboration with Mike, and recipe). Further, without asking—and to stop us from running over one another in our zeal to tell particular stories—he built this matriced edifice of a (*shudder*) spreadsheet that didn't kill me to use. My gratitude knows no bounds, Miguel.

Hellen Die, she of the vaunted Necro-nom-nom-icon *Blog of Dark Foodness* and gourmet extraordinaire, did vouchsafe this tome the unspeakably splendid: Hot Cthocolate, Necronomicorn, Pick Your Brain, Sour Guggies, and There Cannoli Be One recipes. Need something difficult to work and look utterly fantastic? Go to Hellen Die! For anything that I gave up trying to make work or that needed to look spooktacular, Hellen raised her hands. (We think she has eight or so?) How she does what she does in the time she does it, we dare not ask, though we certainly have . . . suspicions. You are amazing, madame, and we are darkly blessed to have you on the team.

Alix Bishoff McDonough literally wandered up to us at a convention and, like any good representative of the Dark Side, handed us cookies. A tome of snacks has to have cookies, right? Yes, and what became the Discs of Wasa'bi and the Café au R'lyeh Cookies came from her inspiration. What's the lesson here? Mike and Tom don't leave the booth during a show, and we *still* don't always remember to pack food. So if you save us from rumbling tummies and hangry mood swings, you might be immortalized in . . . cookie recipes. Who knows? It worked once! Thank you, Alix. You and your recipes are both super fun!

Miss Mina Murray, as she is known in that other book with a face, has been gloriously kind to us with her posts, magnificent photos, and general support. What became Gaunt with the Cinn-ed and the Flats of Ulthar came to us from her and her partner, the ominous and adorably named Mr. Scratch's kitchen, and we were delighted to be able to include them. Given the opportunity, how does one *not* include the headmistress of the Boston Academy of Burlesque Education? Thank you, Miss Mina. You're wonderful!

Chef Velmoor has a delightful YouTube channel that you definitely should check out. He's been cooking from the *Nom* and making wonderful videos. I had the pleasure of meeting him in person at Sci-Fi Valley Con. Of course I asked whether he had something he wanted to see in the book. I hope you like the treatment your spiral-cut chips got, good chef. The Spiraling Madness of Baar'bek-Hu is a fun one for sure.

Sarah Armstrong gifted me with a no-bake margarita cheesecake recipe, oh, probably ten years before *The Necronomnomnom* was even an idea. On your desk, you had a little glass cube that said, "All change is loss." I'm fairly sure you'd be at loss as to how your recipe changed for this book. You have a great sense of humor, so maybe it's OK?

Daniel Slater offered his famous-in-our-house pumpkin pull-apart bread. I'm very pleased with the use I put it to, even if I did have to explain it to him. I don't know why the Mad Arab's fate fascinates me, but this is the second work in which I included it. This one will see publication first, though. Alhazred Pull-Aparts. Delicious. How far you've come from that blank-eyed little boy on page 109 of *The Necronomnomnom*.

How many recipes did Maggie, the Unquestioned Mistress of the Sanctum Savorum, help me test? I lost count. All I know is that I'm ever grateful for her support and forbearance. I've gotten better about the post-ritual clean-up, promise. Her Craisin Dreams are a household favorite, and I'm sorry about what I did to that cookie cutter. Who knew an upside-down snowman could so easily become a skull with a little stretching?

Then there's my Bella, the most adventurous bestest sport ever about trying the weirdness that appears on the kitchen counter. She probably prevented a couple of things from leaving the house that rightly never should have—at least in their original forms.

Kurt Komoda is ever the fearsome guardian and exacting master of visions and spectacles. One day, our photographic skills won't cause him to rail at the sky and the many hells to which he would damn our misbegotten images if he could. In the meantime, we try to improve. His suffering is legendary, but his results are impeccable.

Thomas Roache, the other half of Red Duke Games, chief culinary officer and CEO, culinary wizard, creator and tester of many and various insane ideas, you are a kitchen genie, and your magic sparkles in the darkness of these pages. I've gone well past my allotment of wishes, but you don't seem to be keeping track.

Charlene Roache, Tom's other half, is due all thanks for keeping the children alive and the house running (or, is it the other way around?) while Tom did Tom things for the project and company. Anyone who knows Tom must assign supernatural levels of patience to his mate.

James Jayo, editor, adviser, and to some degree architect of this tome that I wouldn't have thought to create with each of the five tastes in mind. The result? This offering of so many wildly different snacks. Brilliant! Are some shoehorned a bit into some categories? Perhaps, but they work with a little forgiveness and imagination. Certainly we're happy with the results when they hit page or plate. Masters of the Five Tastes, are we? That's a stretch, but we're down that road because of you, James.

INDEX